D1396237

Mental Healthcare Matters in Primary Care

Ruth Chambers
Elizabeth Boath
and
Gill Wakley
With contributions from
Kuljit Jheeta

WITHDRAWN

Foreword by
André Tylee

Staffordshire
UNIVERSITY

RADCLIFFE MEDICAL PRESS

© 2001 Ruth Chambers, Elizabeth Boath and Gill Wakley
Cartoons © 2001 Martin Davies

Radcliffe Medical Press Ltd
18 Marcham Road, Abingdon, Oxon OX14 1AA

British Library Cataloguing in Publication Data

A catalogue record for this book is available from the British Library.

ISBN 1 85775 409 3

Typeset by Joshua Associates Ltd, Oxford
Printed and bound by TJ International Ltd, Padstow, Cornwall

Contents

Foreword

Today's general practitioner needs to be able to recognise, diagnose, assess, manage (with medication and talking treatment) and refer appropriately, anyone who has mental health needs. This is at a time when public expectations have never been so high and there is increasing pressure for faster access to primary care. Mental health is a priority area and the subject of the first National Service Framework, much of the National Plan and an increasing number of national guidelines. As we move towards an increasingly primary care-led NHS, the new primary care organisations are becoming more and more quality driven. Guidance is needed on how to improve the quality of primary mental healthcare in practical terms.

Ruth Chambers is the ideal author of such a book, having devoted her career to the pursuit of quality, training, mental health and stress management. She has developed, with colleagues, an eminently sensible approach to the subject. Of particular note is a model containing 14 core components of professional and service development. These can be applied to personal development plans, practice development plans and clinical governance for each of the main mental health topics. This approach will, I hope, become the benchmark for practitioners and primary care organisations alike which can only benefit consumers with mental health needs.

Professor André Tylee MD FRCGP MRCPsych
Head of Primary Care Mental Health Section
Health Services Research Department
Institute of Psychiatry, and
Guy's, King's and St Thomas' Hospitals
Department of General Practice and Primary Care
King's College, London
May 2001

Preface

A family-centred approach to integrated and community-based mental healthcare

In a typical working day a GP expects a significant psychological component in 70% of consultations. A mental health problem is the sole reason for consultation for 20–25% of patients. Common mental health problems in primary care are characterised by anxiety, depression and somatisation. They are frequently provoked by stress from family relationships, work, social isolation, chronic physical illness or lifestyles such as substance abuse.

These so-called 'worried well' are 'worried sick' and just as disabled as most sufferers of chronic physical diseases,[1] generating major social and financial burdens for their families, friends and employers, and consuming scarce health resources. Even in apparently purely physical conditions such as heart disease, depression increases the risk of sudden death.

Consider that:

- in the UK about 90% of mental healthcare is delivered solely in primary care[2]
- depression accounts for 10% of all new diagnoses in primary care[3]
- antidepressant drugs account for 7% of UK primary care drug expenditure[3]
- primary care is criticised for being unable to recognise and effectively treat mental disorders[4]
- untreated depressed patients use two to three times more of the annual medical services compared with their non-depressed counterparts[5]
- depression is a stronger predictor of serious cardiac disease during the year following cardiac catheterisation than smoking, severity of coronary artery disease and diminished left ventricular ejection fraction.[6]

Primary care provides most of the medical and psychosocial interventions for the majority of patients. Most patients present their problems as undifferentiated mixtures of physical, emotional, family and social symptoms. Yet we continue to organise whole systems of health and social care which separate the biomedical aspects from the psychological and social aspects. The limitation of such a simplistic 'body *or* mind' approach is challenged by several studies of mental disorders in primary care,[7-10] which consistently report the co-occurrence of physical, emotional and social problems in patients. Such patients are also likely to be the highest utilisers of these services.[11]

Consider some of this evidence.

- Only 20% of patients who present with persisting symptoms in primary care have discoverable physical causes, and 10% have clear psychological causes.[12]
- The 10 most common persisting symptoms are fatigue, back pain, dizziness, dyspepsia, cough, insomnia, weight loss, abdominal pain, numbness and constipation. These account for 40% of all GP consultations, and yet one year later only 15% of these cases will have a clearly attributed physical cause.[8]
- The highest 10% of healthcare utilisers use more consultations, as many prescriptions and more consultant referrals than the lowest 50% of utilisers.[11] Of these high utilisers, over half are significantly psychologically distressed. GPs found more than one-third of the high utilisers frustrating to work with in this study, as these patients tended to express their distress in the form of somatisation and anxiety.
- Around 20% of patients attend solely for psychological problems.[13] However, when the role of psychological factors in physical illness is included, this figure increases to 75–80%.[14]
- Around 15–25% of primary care medical decisions that are thought to be made by GPs are based on health morbidity. The remaining decisions are based on psychosocial needs, patient preferences and the doctor–patient relationship.[15]

For each of us, sustaining mental well-being has many facets, including food, warmth and shelter, family and friends, good health, income, education and employment. When threatened by mental distress or illness, the success of any interventions will hinge on our systems of care being able to maintain these fundamental needs. Good mental healthcare will not be achieved until these systems are integrated and based in the communities in which we live. It is unhelpful to separate mental illness into mild *or* severe and to allocate people's care to primary *or* secondary, medical *or* social. This *either/or* approach must be replaced by a *both/and* approach. This forms the basis of a *family-centred approach to integrated and community-based mental healthcare.*

However, much of UK healthcare delivery is characterised by increasing specialisation that uses biomedical models of disease whilst ignoring psychosocial explanations. Primary mental health development has largely been ignored compared with that in specialist care, resulting in shortages of suitably trained primary care professionals, inadequate knowledge of what works in primary care and insufficient protected time for consultations about mental health problems. Many GPs lack confidence in managing mental health issues,[16] perhaps reflecting the fact that only 25% of GPs have held postgraduate psychiatric posts. Yet it is primary healthcare that must address the psychological needs of the vast majority of people. It is inconceivable that this scale of need could ever be met by specialist mental health services. In recognising that such a high proportion of medical care is driven by psychological and social concerns, the ability of the two systems to meet this demand (and costs) will ultimately hinge on their ability to integrate services.[16]

Primary mental healthcare has reached a watershed. We need a model of mental health therapy that is consistent with the goals, strategies and culture of primary care – not imported or translocated models of specialist mental healthcare. Mental healthcare cannot afford to follow simplistic 'body *or* mind', 'physical *or* emotional' approaches to illness. Making the family and socio-environmental information more visible allows the primary care professional to begin to see the connections – and to explain what might previously have been unexplainable when only considering a biomedical model.

Most important of all, our systems of care should understand the limitations of the *either/or* philosophy, which sees diseases as simply *either* biomedical *or* psychosocial. As Alexander Blount[17] points out: 'a smile is as biological as a cancer; it's just that the biological explanation of a smile is rarely needed to explain those aspects of the phenomenon that are important to us.' Thus the paradigm shift that primary care needs is towards a *both/and* philosophy which restores the traditional concept of family practice in the context of the modern primary healthcare team.

Dr David Shiers
West Midlands Primary Care Mental Health Network
GP, Leek, North Staffordshire
May 2001

Editor's Note

Warning! Problems with defining distress as a psychiatric disorder[18]

Other authors have drawn attention to the importance of differentiating between personal distress and psychiatric disorders – as in Derek Summerfield's example of post-traumatic stress disorder. He points out that distress or suffering is not necessarily psychopathology, and that post-traumatic stress disorder is an entity constructed as much from socio-political ideas as from psychiatric ones. He concludes that 'the psychiatric sciences have sought to convert human misery and pain into technical problems that can be understood in standardised ways and are amenable to technical interventions by experts.' He warns that such medicalisation 'tends to mean that distress is relocated from the social arena to the clinical arena . . . [with] practical gains for some, but costs may accrue for everyone over time if contributing factors rooted in political and commercial philosophies and practices escape proper scrutiny'.

References

1 Melzer H, Gill B, Petticrew M and Hinds K (1995) *The Prevalence of Psychiatric Morbidity Among Adults Living in Private Households.* HMSO, London.

2 Goldberg DP and Huxley P (1980) *Mental Illness in the Community: the pathways to psychiatric care.* Tavistock Publications, London.

3 Peveler R, George C, Kinmouth A, Campbell C and Thompson C (1999) Effect of antidepressant drug counselling and information leaflets on adherence to drug treatment in primary care: randomised controlled trial. *BMJ.* **319**: 612–15.

4 Bolestrian S, Williams P and Wilkinson G (1988) Specialist mental health treatment in general practice: a meta-analysis. *Psychol Med.* **18**: 711–17.

5 Simon G, von Korff M and Barlow W (1995) Health care costs of primary care patients with recognised depression. *Arch Gen Psychiatry.* **52**: 850–6.

6 Carney RM, Rich MW, Freedland KE, Saini J and teVelde A (1988) Major depressive disorder predicts cardiac events in patients with coronary artery disease. *Psychosom Med.* **50**: 627–33.

7 Barrett J, Barrett J, Oxman T and Gerber P (1988) The prevalence of psychiatric disorders in primary care practice. *Arch Gen Pract.* **45**: 1100–6.

8 Bridges KW and Goldberg DP (1985) Somatic presentation of DSM-III psychiatric disorders in primary care. *J Psychosom Res.* **29**: 563–9.

9 Kaplan CL, Lipkin M and Gordon G (1988) Somatisation in primary care: patients with unexplained and vexing medical problems. *J Gen Intern Med.* **3**: 177–90.

10 Katon W, von Korff M, Lin E, Lipscomb P, Russo J and Wagner E (1992) A randomised trial of psychiatric consultation with distressed high utilisers. *Gen Hosp Psychiatry.* **14**: 86–98.

11 Katon W, von Korff M, Lin E *et al.* (1990) Distressed high utilisers of medical care: DSM-III-R diagnosis and treatment needs. *Gen Hosp Psychiatry.* **12**: 355–62.

12 Kroenke K and Mangelsdorff AD (1989) Common symptoms in ambulatory care: incidence, evaluation, therapy and outcome. *Am J Med.* **86**: 262–6.

13 Coleman JV (1983) Interdisciplinary implication of primary medical care. In: RS Miller (ed.) *Primary Health Care: more than medicine.* Prentice Hall, Eaglewood Cliffs, NJ.

14 Katon W, von Korff M, Lin E *et al.* (1995) Collaborative management to achieve treatment guidelines: impact on depression in primary care. *JAMA.* **273**: 1026–31.

15 Friedman R, Sobel D, Myers P, Caudill M and Benson H (1995) Behavioural medicine, clinical health psychology and cost offset. *Health Psychol.* **14**: 509–18.

16 Kendrick T, Sibbald B, Burns T and Freeling P (1991) Role of general practitioners in care of long-term mentally ill patients. *BMJ.* **302**: 508–10.

17 Blount A (ed.) (1998). *Primary Integrated Care: the future of medical and mental health collaboration.* W W Norton, London.

18 Summerfield D (2001) The invention of post-traumatic stress disorder and the social usefulness of a psychiatric category. *BMJ.* **322**: 95–8.

About the authors

Ruth Chambers has been a GP for more than 20 years and is currently the Professor of Primary Care Development at the Centre for Health Policy and Practice at Staffordshire University. She has been a GP adviser to a mental health NHS trust for the last two years.

Ruth gained her doctorate from research into the mental and physical health of general practitioners and other professionals. She was a GP Stress Fellow with the Royal College of General Practitioners and the Department of Health in the late 1990s, when her role was to promote ways of overcoming stress in doctors. She has designed and organised many types of educational initiatives, including distance-learning programmes. Recently she has developed a keen interest in working with GPs, nurses and others in primary care around clinical governance and practice personal and professional development plans. This is one of a series of books that Ruth Chambers and Gill Wakley have designed to help readers to draw up their own personal development plans or practice learning plans around important clinical topics such as mental healthcare.

Elizabeth Boath is the Head of the Centre for Health Policy and Practice at the School of Health, Staffordshire University. She has a keen interest in mental health, particularly perinatal mental health, and this is reflected by her extensive publications in this area. She is a member of the West Midlands Primary Mental Health Network. She has a degree in psychology, and her PhD addressed the cost-effectiveness of two alternative approaches to the treatment of postnatal depression. Liz has been involved in health services research for over 14 years as a researcher, research facilitator and lecturer. She has taught on a wide range of topics, including critical appraisal skills, evidence-based practice, clinical governance and clinical effectiveness.

Gill Wakley started in general practice in 1966, but transferred to community medicine shortly afterwards and then into public health. A desire for increased contact with patients caused her to move back into general practice, together with community gynaecology, in 1978. She has been combining the two, in varying amounts, ever since.

Throughout she has been heavily involved in learning and teaching. She was in a training general practice, became an instructing doctor and a regional assessor in family planning, and was until recently a Senior Clinical Lecturer with the Primary Care Department at Keele University, Staffordshire. Like Ruth, she has run all types of educational initiatives and activities, from individual mentoring and instruction to small group work, plenary lectures, distance-learning programmes, workshops, and courses for a wide range of health professionals and lay people.

Kuljit Jheeta is a health economist who is completing her PhD on dementia at the Centre for Health Policy and Practice, under the supervision of Ruth Chambers. She has been investigating how GPs and community nurses diagnose and classify people as having dementia, from the perspectives of health professionals, patients and their carers.

Acknowledgements

We should like to thank the medical librarians, Irene Fenton and David Rogers, from the North Staffordshire Medical Institute for their unfailing help. The Foundation NHS Trust in Stafford has enhanced our understanding of best practice in mental healthcare and provides a good example of how those working in a Mental Health Trust can work closely together with those in primary care, in order to co-ordinate care and services around patients' needs.

Introduction

Blend your continuing professional development with national requirements to improve mental healthcare

The material in this book sets out how learning more about mental healthcare and reviewing current practice can be incorporated into your personal development plan, whether you are a GP, a practice nurse, a practice manager or any other member of the primary care team.

This is not a comprehensive book on mental healthcare. We offer a selection of common topics as examples of how to explore best practice in mental healthcare, and we will show you how to apply that best practice using clinical governance through continuing professional development.

You need to develop a dual focus on improving the management of mental healthcare and increasing the efficiency of the working environment in the general practice. Practice team members should work together to direct their individual learning plans to form their practice personal and professional development plan. This should complement the business plan of the practice or primary care group/primary care trust in England, the local health group in Wales, the local healthcare co-operative in Scotland or the primary care co-operative in Northern Ireland. These organisations will be referred to as primary care organisations (PCOs) throughout the rest of the book.

The reason for focusing on mental health is that ill health problems are common, and many of them are not diagnosed. Your personal development plan should enable you to learn how to provide the standards of care that are set out in the National Service Framework (NSF) for Mental Health for England[1] and other national initiatives.

The NSFs for England incorporate integrated packages of care and give a clinical focus for the strategic development of health services. NSFs should improve standards and the quality of care, and reduce variations in services.[2] The national standards set out in the NSF for Mental Health for England will be delivered locally through clinical governance and health improvement programmes. Delivery is underpinned by professional self-regulation, research and development into effective interventions, and human resources programmes. The Centre for Health Improvement (CHI), the NHS Performance Framework and the NHS Patient Survey will monitor the standards. The NSFs have a strong patient focus, including provision of good information, opportunities for patients to participate in decision making, and more transparency about service quality and outcomes.

You may decide to allocate 50% of the time you intend to spend on your personal development plan in any one year, on learning more about mental healthcare. That would leave space in your learning plan for other important topics such as diabetes, coronary heart disease or cancer – whatever is a priority for you, your practice team and your patient population. There will be some overlap between topics. For example, you cannot consider a person with dementia in isolation. You need to look at any coexisting depression and at the needs of their carers, who may have depression, anxiety or stress, too.

The first chapter of the book describes how a clinical governance culture incorporates effective clinical management and well-organised working conditions. You should be able to demonstrate that you are fit to practise as an individual clinician or manager, and that your working environment is fit to practise from. This section will be relevant to all healthcare staff so that you understand more of the context within which you work and how your individual contribution fits into the whole picture of healthcare.

The following chapters cover the evidence for the modern management of some aspects of mental health. We usually cite evidence from a review or compendium rather than the original literature.

The whole programme builds up to the generation of personal development plans in Chapter 8 and a practice personal and professional development plan in Chapter 9. These are presented as worked examples of personal development plans in *stress management* and *dementia*, and a practice personal and professional development plan focusing on *depression*. Each of these chapters has an empty template for you to photocopy and complete for your own personal development plan or for your practice team's personal and professional development plan. There are worked examples of other topics in our associated books[3,4] and other clinical topics in this series, or you can download the learning plan templates from www.primarycareonline.co.uk.

Reflection exercises at the end of each chapter give the reader an opportunity to assess their learning needs, review their performance or that of the practice organisation, and reflect on what improvements to make. You should transfer information from these needs assessment exercises to the relevant slots in your personal development plan as an individual, or your practice personal and professional development plan if you are working as a team. Adopt a wide-based approach to improving quality – think of how you are establishing a clinical governance culture in your own practice team through your timed action plans.

What should you do next?

Study the templates for a personal development plan or a practice personal and professional development plan on pages 151–181. You will be filling one in as you go along. Will you start out on your personal development plan or work with colleagues on the practice learning plan? Everyone's personal development plans should mesh with the practice learning plan.

Having worked through the book and associated exercises, you will be able to make changes – to your workplace, or to the equipment in your practice, or to the advice you give patients, or to the way in which you manage mental illness and other mental health disorders.

References

1 Barton S (ed.) (2001) *Clinical Evidence. Issue 5*. BMJ Publishing Group, London.
2 Wilkinson G, Moore B and Moore P (2000) *Treating People with Depression*. Radcliffe Medical Press, Oxford.
3 Chambers R and Wakley G (2000) *Making Clinical Governance Work for You*. Radcliffe Medical Press, Oxford.
4 Wakley G, Chambers R and Field S (2000) *Continuing Professional Development: making it happen*. Radcliffe Medical Press, Oxford.

CHAPTER 1

Clinical governance and mental healthcare

Clinical governance is about doing anything and everything required to maximise the quality of healthcare or services, including care and services for those with mental health problems.[1]

The Commission for Health Improvement (CHI) defines clinical governance as 'the framework through which NHS organisations and their staff are accountable for the quality of patient care.'[2]

CHI's perspective of clinical governance includes the following:

- a patient-centred approach which treats patients with courtesy, involves them in decisions and keeps them informed
- an accountability for quality which ensures that clinical care is up to date in general practices
- ensuring high standards and safety
- improvement in patient services and care.

We can use clinical governance to improve the detection and management of mental health problems. Clinical governance is inclusive, making quality everyone's business, whether they are a doctor, a nurse or other health professional, a manager, a member of staff or a strategic planner. Good mental healthcare relies on the multidisciplinary team to support the person with mental health problems in self-managing their disease inasmuch as they are able to do so. Delivering best practice requires sufficient clinical staff who are up to date and relate well to their patients, and efficient systems and procedures that are patient friendly.[3]

Components of clinical governance

The components of clinical governance are not new. However, bringing them together under the banner of clinical governance and introducing more explicit accountability for performance is a new style of working.[1,3]

The following 14 themes are core components of professional and service development which together form a comprehensive approach to providing high-quality healthcare services and clinical governance.[1] These are illustrated in Figure 1.1.

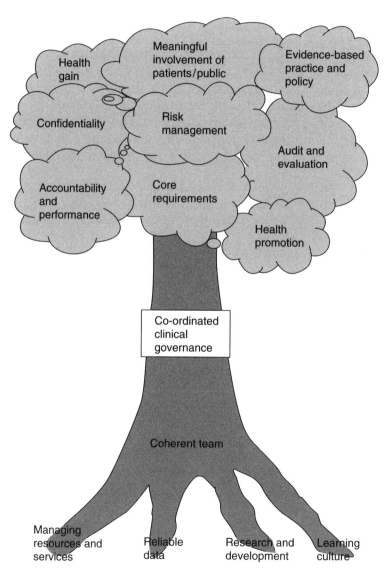

Figure 1.1: 'Routes' and branches of clinical governance.

If you interweave these 14 components into your individual and practice learning plans you will have addressed the requirements for clinical governance at the same time.[1,3]

1 *Learning culture*: for patients and staff in the practice or primary care organisation, or in secondary care.
2 *Research and development culture*: in the practice or throughout the health service.
3 *Reliable and accurate data*: in the practice, and across the primary care organisation and the NHS as a seamless whole.
4 *Well-managed resources and services*: as individuals, as a practice, across the NHS and in conjunction with other organisations.
5 *Coherent team*: well-integrated teams within a practice, including attached staff such as community psychiatric nurses, counsellors and other community nurses.
6 *Meaningful involvement of patients and the public*: including those with mental health problems, those who care for them and the general population.
7 *Health gain*: from improving the health of staff and patients in a practice, between practices and within a primary care organisation.
8 *Confidentiality*: of information in consultations, in medical notes and between practitioners.
9 *Evidence-based practice and policy*: applying it in practice, in the district and across the NHS.
10 *Accountability and performance*: for standards, performance of individuals and the practice, both to the public and to those in authority.
11 *Core requirements*: good fit with skill mix and whether individuals are competent to do their jobs; communication, workforce numbers and morale at practice level.
12 *Health promotion*: for patients, the public, your staff and colleagues – both opportunistic and in general, or targeting those with most needs.
13 *Audit and evaluation*: for instance, of the extent to which individuals and primary care teams adhere to best practice in clinical management.
14 *Risk management*: being competent to detect those at risk, and reducing the risks and probabilities of ill health. This is particularly important in mental healthcare, where untreated conditions such as depression and psychoses can have serious consequences.

The challenges to delivering clinical governance

Delivering high-quality healthcare with guaranteed minimum standards of care at all times is a major challenge. At present, the quality of healthcare is patchy and variable. We are not very good at detecting under-performance and rectifying it at an early stage. The small number of clinicians who do under-perform exert a disproportionately large effect on the public's confidence. Causes of under-performance in an individual might be a result of a lack of knowledge or skills, poor attitudes, ill health or a lack of resources. A lack of management capability is nearly always a contributory reason for inadequate clinical services.

We need to understand why variation exists and explore ways of reducing inequalities. Variation in the quality of healthcare provided is common – between different practices in the same locality, between staff of the same discipline working in the same practice or unit, and between care given to some groups of the population rather than others. For instance, not all practices have written guidelines for referral of patients with mental health problems such as dementia, and patients in some practices have easy access to a community psychiatric nurse that others do not have.

Clinical governance offers a co-ordinated approach to overcoming these areas of risk. The complex cultural change that will be required to deliver uniformly excellent care is immense. We need to develop measurable outcomes that professionals, patients and the public consider to be relevant and meaningful. Then we can assess the progress made through implementing clinical governance in the standards set out in the National Service Framework (NSF) for Mental Health for England and other national and locally planned programmes across the UK.[4]

Learning culture

Education and training programmes should be relevant to service needs, whether at organisational or individual levels. Continuing professional development (CPD) programmes need to meet both the learning needs of individual health professionals and the wider service development needs of the NHS. You should no longer opt for CPD activities according to what you *want* to do, but rather according to what you *need* to do. Clinical governance underpins professional and service development.

Box 1.1

Individual personal development plans
will feed into a
practice-based personal and professional development plan
that will feed into
the practice's/primary care organisation's business plan
all of which are
underpinned by clinical governance.[1,3]

Multidisciplinary learning will boost close teamwork when providing mental healthcare. Service users can have a useful input into interprofessional education, as the illustration in Box 1.2 shows.

Box 1.2 Partnerships with service users in interprofessional education for community mental health[5]

Participants in one multidisciplinary training initiative valued users' contributions to their learning programme very highly. The staff participating were from health, social services and voluntary organisations working with people in the community who have severe mental illness.

Service users were an integral part of the panel who commissioned the educational programme. Users contributed to teaching sessions individually with professionals, and helped in the planning and design of some modules. A user perspective was also incorporated into the expected learning outcomes of the course. Workshops developed users' training skills.

Any new educational approaches should be critically evaluated to determine whether there are any actual health benefits for patients, as the example in Box 1.3 illustrates.

Box 1.3 Outcome of depressed patients was no different after practice team education[6]

Education was delivered to 60 multidisciplinary practice teams to enhance their recognition of depression in a randomised controlled trial. The education was well received by participants, 80% of whom believed that it would change their management of patients with depression. The education did not increase the sensitivity or the specificity of doctors' recognition of depression, and there was no improvement in recovery rates of the patients identified through screening.

Applying research and development in practice

The findings of the many thousands of research papers about mental ill health conditions that are published in reputable journals each year are rarely applied in practice. This is because few health professionals or managers read such journals regularly, and therefore they are unaware of the research findings. Most practice teams do not have a system for reviewing important research papers and translating that review into practical action.

A primary care organisation might help by feeding important new evidence to its constituent practices or pharmacies, or to the general public. Improvements should result if local disease templates for recording data and making changes to working practices can be agreed and backed with resources (e.g. templates for depression, dementia, psychoses).

Box 1.4

Incorporating research-based evidence into everyday practice should promote policies on effective working, improve quality and create a clinical governance culture.

Research increases our understanding of the causes and effects of mental health problems as well as enabling the development of new treatments. For example, people with a 'dual' diagnosis have a severe mental illness such as schizophrenia, depression or manic depression, *and* a severe drug or alcohol problem. One large research study in the USA found that 47% of people with schizophrenia abused drugs or alcohol, too. The mental illness may have developed first, or it may follow an alcohol or drug problem. Other research comparing individuals who had a dual diagnosis with others who had a psychosis alone found that those with a dual diagnosis are more often younger, male and at higher risk of homelessness.[7]

Reliable and accurate data

Table 1.1 Some Read codes for key conditions in mental healthcare

Abbreviation	Code
Alcohol dependence	
Alcohol dependence syndrome	E23
Chronic alcoholism	E231
Anxiety states	
Anxiety states	E200
Generalised anxiety	E2002
Panic disorder	E2001
Obsessive-compulsive disorder	E2141
Compulsive personality disorder	E214
Depression (single)	
Single major depressive episode	E112
Mild (single episode)	E1121
Moderate (single episode)	E1122
Severe (single episode)	E1123
Psychosis (single episode)	E1124
Depression (recurrent)	
Recurrent major depressive episode	E113
Mild (recurrent episode)	E1131
Moderate (recurrent episode	E1132
Severe (recurrent episode)	E1133
Psychosis (recurrent episode)	E1134
Mania	
Mania (single episode)	E110
Mania (recurrent episode)	E111
Schizophrenia	
Schizophrenic disorders	E10
Stress	
Acute reaction to stress	E28

Clinicians, patients and administrators need access to reliable and accurate data. Set the following standards for a general practice.

- Keep records in chronological order.
- Summarise medical records, within specified time period for records of new patients.
- Review dates for checks on medication, with audit in place to monitor whether standards are adhered to, and to plan for under-performance if necessary.
- Use computers for diagnostic recording, and agree Read codes for different classifications of mental ill health conditions.
- Record information from external sources (e.g. hospital, other organisations) that is relevant to individual patients or the practice.
- Keep good written records of policies and audits that relate to various types of mental ill health in the practice.

An inspection at any time should show what audits have been undertaken and when, the changes in practice organisation that followed, the extent of staff training undertaken, and the future programme of monitoring.

Box 1.5 Suicide rate is decreasing[8]

The Office of National Statistics keeps accurate records that follows population trends and will contribute to monitoring the effect of the national targets to reduce suicide (*see* Chapter 2 for more information).

The rise in the suicide rate in men in England and Wales in the 1970s and 1980s has reversed. The suicide rate and 'undetermined' death rate for both men and women have been steadily decreasing since 1990 for all age groups. The frequency of suicide by hanging and strangulation has increased in men, whilst poisoning by gases and vapours, including car-exhaust fumes, was found to be less often used by both men and women.

Well-managed resources and services

The things you need to achieve best practice should be in the right place at the right time, and working correctly every time.

Set standards in your practice or workplace for the following:

- access to premises and availability of services for people with special needs (e.g. those whose confidence has been sapped by mental health problems)
- provision of routine and urgent appointments (e.g. for those with depression)
- access to and provision for referral for investigation or treatment
- pro-active monitoring of chronic illness and disability
- alternatives to face-to-face consultations
- consultation length.

The primary care services to which the public requires access include information, advice, triage and treatment, continuity of care, personal care and other services.

Box 1.6

Mental health is a key priority in Scotland's Public Health White Paper *Towards a Healthier Scotland* and the NHS White Paper *Designed to Care*. Scottish GPs are calling for support to be given to the 'greater integration of mental health services within primary care, including the availability and provision of services out of hours'. They see mental healthcare as being more community orientated, with mental health specialists (e.g. psychiatrists and community psychiatric nurses) and special services supporting rather than substituting for primary care.[9]

Systems should be designed to prevent and detect errors. Therefore keep systems simple and sensible, and inform everyone how those systems operate so that they are less likely to bypass a system or make errors. Establish good systems for the follow-up of patients with depression, dementia or psychoses.

Coherent teamwork

Teams do produce better patient care than single practitioners operating in a fragmented way. Effective teams make the most of the different contributions of individual clinical disciplines in delivering patient care. The characteristics of effective teams are as follows:

- shared ownership of a common purpose
- clear goals for the contributions that each discipline makes
- open communication between team members
- opportunities for team members to enhance their skills.[1]

A team approach helps different team members to adopt an evidence-based approach to patient care – by having to justify their approach to the rest of the team. The disciplines necessary for providing team-based mental healthcare include the GP, the practice nurse and other community nurses, non-clinical staff, the community psychiatric nurse, the psychologist, the community pharmacist, social carers, and support workers from not-for-profit agencies, with help from other expert health professionals (e.g. the psychiatrist).

Box 1.7

The National Service Framework for Mental Health for England urges primary care to develop and implement protocols with other sectors to manage common mental health problems. These will include depression as the first priority, then postnatal depression, eating disorders, anxiety disorders and schizophrenia. Such protocols will require all of the team to be certain of, and trained for, their roles and responsibilities in planning and delivering care and services.[4]

Meaningful involvement of patients and the public

Box 1.8

'I was no longer a being with feelings, ideas, beliefs, points of view or a future. All I was, was the recipient of a specific drug, and that was it.'

Andy from Luton[10]

People use terms like 'user' or 'consumer' to describe who they should be involving in giving feedback about the quality or type of healthcare on offer, or in planning future services. Patients or carers, non-users of services, the local community, a particular subgroup of the population or the general public will all have useful feedback and views (e.g. on your systems that inform people about the results of investigations, or locating services closer to the patient).

Box 1.9

'People experiencing mental illness are the best sources of information for and about people with mental illness.'

Steve from Belfast[10]

The aims of user involvement and public participation include better outcomes of individual care, better health of the population, more locally responsive services and greater ownership of health services. Those planning the services should develop a better understanding of why and how local services need to be changed. For example, you might want to consult the public and health professionals about the closure of a community hospital, without which those with chronic conditions may have to travel further for their care.

Box 1.10 What do carers of patients with dementia expect from GPs?

Ask carers this question and they will give the following answers:

- assessment and diagnosis of the patient with dementia
- information about the illness, what symptoms and signs to expect, and what treatments exist
- referral to social services in as bureaucracy-free a way as possible
- up-to-date information about the availability of new drugs, and how to access drug trials
- help for carers – with understanding of and empathy with their damaged family relationships
- practical help in accessing services and support.

Shirley, whose husband has dementia[11]

Health gain

The two general approaches to improving health are the 'population' approach, which focuses on measures to improve health through the community, and the 'high-risk' approach, which focuses on vulnerable individuals who are at high risk of the condition or hazard. We generally

use a targeted approach to identify individuals whose depression or psychosis was previously undiagnosed, rather than undertaking population screening.

The two approaches are not mutually exclusive, and they often need to be combined with legislation and community action. Health goals include:

- a good quality of life
- avoiding premature death
- equal opportunities for health.[1]

Standard 1 of the National Service Framework for Mental Health for England consists of a population approach targeted both at communities and at individuals at risk. For example, health visitors target new mothers for the prevention, identification and management of postnatal depression.

Box 1.11 Standard 1[4]

Health and social services should:

- promote mental health for all, working with individuals and communities
- combat discrimination against individuals and groups with mental health problems, and promote their social inclusion.

Confidentiality

Confidentiality is a component of clinical governance that is often overlooked. Experienced health professionals and managers may assume that junior or new staff know all about confidentiality when in fact they may not. There are many difficult situations in the NHS where one person asks for information about another individual's medical condition where it is not clear-cut as to whether this information should be supplied or withheld, or even if it should be acknowledged that the person being enquired about is receiving care. For instance, there comes a stage when it is reasonable for a health professional to divulge information about a person with progressively deteriorating dementia without the patient's knowledge, but this situation needs to be openly established in discussion with everyone involved.

The Caldicott Committee Report describes the following principles of good practice to safeguard confidentiality when information is being used for non-clinical purposes.[12]

- Justify the purpose.
- Do not use patient-identifiable information unless it is absolutely necessary to do so.
- Use the minimum necessary patient-identifiable information.
- Access to patient-identifiable information should be on a strict need-to-know basis.
- Everyone with access to patient-identifiable information should be aware of his or her responsibilities.

Evidence-based culture – policy and practice

The key features that determined whether or not local guidelines worked in one initiative were that:[13]

- there was multidisciplinary involvement in drawing them up
- a systematic review of the literature underpinned the guidelines, with graded recommendations for best practice linked to the evidence
- there was ownership at national and local levels
- a local implementation plan ensured that the needs for resources, time, staff, education and training were foreseen, met and supported
- plans were made to sustain the guidelines – which were user friendly and could be modified to suit individual practitioners and patients.

Box 1.12

One review of the extent to which existing guidelines are evidence based found that only one-third of those for the management of depression conformed to national quality standards for clinical guidelines.[14]

The hierarchy of evidence that is used to describe how scientifically a particular study was conducted, and therefore how reliable the conclusions are likely to be, varies between different reviews of published studies. There are several systems of grading evidence.

One classification[15] that is often used gives the strength of evidence as shown in Box 1.13.

Box 1.13 Strength of evidence

Type 1   Strong evidence from at least one systematic review of multiple well-designed randomised controlled trials (RCTs)

Type II   Strong evidence from at least one properly designed randomised controlled trial of appropriate size

Type III Evidence from well-designed trials without randomisation, single group pre–post, cohort, time-series or matched case–control studies

Type IV   Evidence from well-designed non-experimental studies from more than one centre or research group

Type V   Opinions of respected authorities, based on clinical evidence, descriptive studies or reports of expert committees

---

Other categories of evidence are listed in the compendium of the best available evidence for effective healthcare – *Clinical Evidence* – which is updated every six months, and is perhaps more useful to the health professional in everyday work (*see* Box 1.14).[16]

Box 1.14

Beneficial	Interventions whose effectiveness has been shown by clear evidence from controlled trials
Likely to be beneficial	Interventions for which effectiveness is less well established than for those listed under 'beneficial'
Trade-off between benefits and harm	Interventions for which clinicians and patients should weigh up the beneficial and harmful effects according to individual circumstances and priorities
Unknown effectiveness	Interventions for which there are currently insufficient data, or data of inadequate quality (this includes interventions that are widely accepted as beneficial but which have never been formally tested in RCTs, often because the latter would be regarded as unethical)

Unlikely to be beneficial	Interventions for which the lack of effectiveness is less well established than for those listed under 'likely to be ineffective or harmful'
Likely to be ineffective or harmful	Interventions whose ineffectiveness or harmfulness has been demonstrated by clear evidence

In this book, when we describe an intervention as being 'effective', we are inferring that there is *Type I* or *Type II* evidence, or that the intervention is 'beneficial' or likely to be beneficial.

Accountability and performance

Health professionals may not always realise that they are accountable to others from outside their own professions, especially if they are of self-employed status, as are GPs, pharmacists and optometrists. However, in fact they are accountable to:

• the general public
• the profession – to maintain the standards of knowledge and skills of the profession as a whole
• the government – and employer – who expect high standards of healthcare from the work-force.

Box 1.15

Health professionals who believe that they are not accountable to others may be reluctant to collect the evidence to demonstrate that they are fit to practise, and that their working environment is fit to practise from. They may be reluctant to co-operate with central NHS requirements, such as contributing to the local health improvement programme or working to the standards set out in the National Service Frameworks.

Identify and rectify under-performance at an early stage by, for example:

• regular appraisals (at least annually) linked to clinical governance and personal development plans as a process of regular supportive meetings between manager and staff member

- detecting those who have significant health problems, and referring them for help
- systematic audit that distinguishes individuals' performance from the overall performance of the practice team
- an open learning culture in which team members are discouraged from covering up colleagues' inadequacies, so that problems can be resolved at an early stage.

Clinicians may regard the performance assessment framework as a management tool that is not particularly relevant to their clinical practice. However, it does reinforce a clinical governance culture whereby good clinical management and organisational management have a symbiotic relationship.

Box 1.16

The NHS performance assessment framework has six components, namely health improvement, fair access, efficiency, effective delivery of appropriate care, user/carer experience and health outcomes.

Health promotion

People with mental health problems benefit if they are well informed about their condition and able to participate in making decisions about the management of their condition. Good information will help patients with various types of mental ill health to make choices about their diet, smoking, physical activity and other health-related behaviour.

Health promotion among the work-force is key to maintaining morale. Organise working arrangements so that the staff are able to take regular breaks from the front desk, and GPs do not take work home. Encourage exercise as part of a well-balanced lifestyle for staff by providing bicycle racks at the surgery, or negotiate reduced membership fees of local health and leisure facilities.

Alcohol plays a significant role in 15–30% of male admissions and 8–15% of female admissions to general hospitals. As many as 75% of hazardous and harmful drinkers are not known to their GPs. New cases can be picked up in primary care by screening opportunistically (e.g. new patient registrations, elderly people at annual checks) or when patients present with physical conditions in which alcohol might be implicated (these include gastrointestinal, cardiovascular, genito-urinary, neurological, dermatological and psychiatric conditions).[17]

The recommended safe limits for drinking are 21 units of alcohol per week for men and 14 units of alcohol per week for women. The CAGE questionnaire, designed to detect 'at-risk' drinking, is shown in Box 1.17. It is simple to administer – two positive answers indicate a high probability of alcohol dependence.[17]

Box 1.17 CAGE enquiry[17]

- Have you ever felt that you should **C**ut down on your drinking?
- Have people **A**nnoyed you by criticising your drinking?
- Have you ever felt bad or **G**uilty about your drinking?
- Have you ever had a drink first thing in the morning to steady your nerves (an **E**ye-opener)?

Audit and evaluation

Follow-up of patients with depression, dementia or psychoses is essential to ensure that they are encouraged to take prescribed medication, or pursue an agreed self-management plan, and that their carers are supported. Audit is the key to checking that patients adhere to their treatment and professionals work according to best practice.

A significant event audit after a suicide or parasuicide can reveal aspects of care that you and other primary healthcare team members might improve. Could you have intervened in any way? Could you work more closely with community mental health teams or others employed by the mental health trust?

Box 1.18

The Department of Health has been tracking popular attitudes to mental illness since 1993. The triennial survey of 2000 adults has shown a small but significant shift in the public's attitudes. In the year 2000, just under 20% of respondents were 'frightened' to think of people with mental illness living in residential areas, compared to 25% in 1997.

Around 90% agreed that we need to 'adopt a far more tolerant attitude towards people with mental illness in our society', 83% disagreed that 'people with a mental illness are a burden on society' (a significant increase from disagreement by 3% in 1997), and 92% believed that virtually anyone can become mentally ill.[18]

This book is mainly concerned with adult mental healthcare, although much of the recommended good practice can be generalised to the care of children and adolescents with mental health disorders. A recent evaluation of the mental health of children and adolescents in England and Wales was conducted in order to determine up-to-date baseline information about the prevalence of mental disorders among 5- to 15-year-olds. The results are shown in Box 1.19.

Box 1.19 Prevalence of mental health disorders in 5- to 15-year-olds[19]

More than 10 000 children and adolescents were studied by interviewing parents and assessing the child concerned, and an associated questionnaire was completed by the child's teacher.

Overall, 10% of children had at least one mental health disorder:

- 5% had clinically significant conduct disorders
- 4% had emotional disorders – anxiety and depression
- 1% were hyperactive
- 0.5% had autistic disorders, tics or eating disorders.

Mental disorder was more common in boys (11%) than in girls (8%). Nearly 10% of white children and 12% of black children had a mental health problem. The prevalence rates among Asian children were 8% of the Pakistani and Bangladeshi children and adolescents and 4% of the Indian children and adolescents sampled.

Children of lone parents were twice as likely to have a mental health problem as those living with married or cohabiting couples (16%, compared with 8%). Mental disorders were more common among 'reconstituted' families where there was at least one step-child living in the family unit, and mental disorder was more common (15%) in reconstituted families than in those that were not (9%). Children of interviewed parents with no educational qualifications were more likely to have a mental health disorder (15%) than those whose interviewed parent had at least a degree-level qualification (6%).

Around 20% of children in families without a working parent had a mental health disorder, compared with 8% of children with at least one working member in the family.

Core requirements

Mental illness costs £32 billion in England each year – taking into account £12 billion in lost employment and £8 billion in benefit payments.[20]

You cannot deliver clinical governance without well-trained and competent staff, the right skill mix of staff, a safe and comfortable working environment and the provision of cost-effective care.

A clinical governance culture addresses the recent challenges[21] in relation to the following:

- *partnership*: working together across the NHS to ensure the best possible care
- *performance*: acting to review and deliver higher standards of healthcare
- *the professions and wider work-force*: breaking down barriers between different disciplines (e.g. through multidisciplinary team-work between GPs, nurses, pharmacists and optometrists)
- *patient care*: access, convenient services, and empowerment to take a full part in decision making about their own medical care and in planning and providing health services in general
- *prevention*: promoting healthy living across all sections of society and tackling variations in care.

All of these components need to be in place to meet the standards set out in the National Service Framework. Those most relevant to primary care are standards 2 and 3 (*see* Box 1.20).

Box 1.20

Standard 2[4]

Any service user who contacts their primary healthcare team with a common mental health problem should:

- have their mental health needs identified and assessed
- be offered effective treatments, including referral to specialist services for further assessment, treatment and care if they require it.

Standard 3[4]

Any individual with a common mental health problem should:

- be able to make contact round the clock with the local services necessary to meet their needs and receive adequate care
- be able to use *NHS Direct*, as it develops, for first-level advice and referral on to specialist helplines or to local services.

In order to achieve standards 2 and 3, each primary healthcare team will 'need to work with specialist mental health services to:

- develop the resources in each practice to assess mental health needs
- develop the resources to work with diverse groups in the population
- develop the skills and competencies to manage common mental health problems
- agree the arrangements for referral for assessment, advice or treatment and care
- have the skills and necessary organisational arrangements to provide the physical healthcare and other primary care support needed, as agreed in their care plan, for patients with a severe mental illness'.[4]

Risk management

People may underestimate relative risks as applied to themselves and their own behaviour – for example, many people accept the relationship between bereavement and depression, but do not believe that they personally are at risk. People usually have a reasonable idea of the *relative risks* of various activities and behaviours, although their personal estimates of the *magnitude* of those risks tend to be biased – small probabilities are often over-estimated and high probabilities are often under-estimated.[22]

Risk management in general practice mainly centres on assessing probabilities that potential or actual hazards will give rise to harm. Consider how bad the risk is, how likely the risk is, when the risk will occur, if ever, and how certain you are of estimates about the risk. This applies just as much whether the risk is an environmental or organisational risk within the practice, or a clinical risk.

Good practice means understanding and managing risk (both clinical and organisational aspects). Undertaking audit more systematically will reduce the risks of omission. Common areas of risk in providing healthcare services include:[22]

- out-of-date clinical practice
- lack of continuity of care
- poor communication
- mistakes in patient care
- patient complaints
- financial risk – insufficient resources
- reputation
- staff morale.

Communicating and managing risks on an individual basis with patients depends on finding ways to explain risks and elicit people's values and preferences. They can then make decisions themselves to take risks or choose between alternatives that involve different risks and benefits.

The major risk factors for mental illness include:[23]

- poverty, poor education and unemployment
- social isolation stemming from discrimination against people with all types of physical disabilities
- major events such as bereavement, redundancy, financial problems or being the victim of crime
- genetic predisposition
- drug and alcohol misuse
- developmental factors such as fetal damage and injury at birth
- poor parenting.

Box 1.21

There is a clear association between risky sexual behaviour and common psychiatric disorders in young people (e.g. anxiety, depression, eating disorders, substance dependence, antisocial disorder, mania, schizophrenia). We need to co-ordinate healthcare for adolescents and young people to cover psychological, sexual and social aspects.[24] There are problems in some areas of the country with regard to adolescents aged 16 or 17 years accessing mental healthcare, where neither the adult nor child healthcare sectors accept this age group as their responsibility. The recent House of Commons Health Committee report has made several recommendations for redressing the current situation to improve services.[25]

Reflection exercise

Exercise 1 (for all members of the practice team)

Review and plan the mental healthcare that you provide.

Think how you might integrate the 14 components of clinical governance into your personal development plan or your practice personal and professional development plan. Examples are given for each component listed below. Complete this yourself from your own perspective.

- *Establishing a learning culture*: e.g. informal discussion about guidelines for primary mental healthcare between GPs, nurses and the community psychiatric nurse.
- *Managing resources and services*: e.g. review the roles and responsibilities for the management of depression by members of the practice team and attached staff.
- *Establishing a research and development culture*: e.g. share among the practice team findings in key research papers on best practice when managing dementia amongst the practice team.
- *Reliable and accurate data*: e.g. keep electronic records (both individual and team) so that everyone uses the same Read codes and enters data consistently. Any audit exercises can be repeated next year and the results compared.
- *Evidence-based practice and policy*: e.g. update the evidence-based protocol or integrated care pathway for managing dementia.
- *Confidentiality*: e.g. review to ensure that everyone is adhering to the agreed code of practice for giving results or advice at the reception desk.
- *Health gain:* e.g. target those with depression for particular efforts in relieving physical symptoms.
- *Coherent team*: e.g. communicate to the rest of the practice team new systems for managing the various types of mental health problems.
- *Audit and evaluation*: e.g. undertake audit and act on the findings to improve the quality of care of those with dementia.
- *Meaningful involvement of patients and the public*: e.g. listen to and act on the comments of those with mental health problems about the care and services that you are providing.
- *Health promotion*: e.g. obtain or write literature promoting physical activity via local walks to help people with mild to moderate depression.
- *Risk management*: e.g. establish systems and procedures to identify, analyse and control clinical risks such as those arising from careless repeat-prescribing practices.
- *Accountability and performance*: e.g. keep good records of those with psychoses to demonstrate best practice in their ongoing management.
- *Core requirements*: e.g. agree roles and responsibilities in the team, such as nurse referral to GPs, and train receptionists in how to act in a crisis situation.

Now that you have completed this interactive reflection exercise, transfer the information about your learning needs to the empty template of the personal development plan on pages 151–161 if you are working on your own learning plan, or to the practice personal and professional development plan on pages 174–181 if you are working on a practice team learning plan. Don't forget to keep the evidence of your learning in your personal portfolio.

References

1 Chambers R and Wakley G (2000) *Making Clinical Governance Work For You.* Radcliffe Medical Press, Oxford.
2 Commission for Health Improvement (2000) *Clinical Governance Reviews. An overview.* Commission for Health Improvement, London.
3 Wakley G, Chambers R and Field S (2000) *Continuing Professional Development: making it happen.* Radcliffe Medical Press, Oxford.
4 NHS Executive (1999) *National Service Framework for Mental Health.* Department of Health, London.
5 Barnes D, Carpenter J and Bailey D (2000) Partnerships with service users in interprofessional education for community mental health: a case study. *J Interprof Care.* **14**: 189–200.
6 Thompson C, Kinmonth AL, Stevens L *et al.* (2000) Effects of a clinical practice guideline and practice-based education on detection and outcome of depression in primary care: Hampshire Depression Project randomised controlled trial. *Lancet.* **355**: 185–91.
7 National Schizophrenia Fellowship (1998) *Dual Diagnosis: mental illness and drug/alcohol problems.* Factsheet 7. National Schizophrenia Fellowship, Kingston upon Thames.
8 Yarney G (2000) Suicide rate is decreasing in England and Wales. *BMJ.* **320**: 75.
9 Royal College of General Practitioners (Scotland) and Scottish General Practitioners Committee (2000) *Valuing Scottish General Practice.* Royal College of General Practitioners, Edinburgh.
10 National Schizophrenia Fellowship, MIND and Manic Depression Fellowship (2000) *A Question of Choice.* National Schizophrenia Fellowship, Kingston upon Thames.
11 Nurock S (2000) GPs – we need you! *J Dementia Care.* **Sept/Oct**: 26–7.
12 Department of Health (1997) Report of the review of patient-identifiable information. In: *The Caldicott Committee Report.* Department of Health, London.
13 Donald P (2000) Promoting local ownership of guidelines. *Guidelines Pract.* **3**: 17.

14 Cornwall P and Scott J (2000) Which clinical practice guidelines for depression? An overview for busy practitioners. *Br J Gen Pract.* **50**: 908–11.
15 Muir Gray JA (1997) *Evidence-Based Healthcare.* Churchill Livingstone, Edinburgh.
16 Barton S (ed.) (2001) *Clinical Evidence. Issue 5.* BMJ Publishing Group, London.
17 Feeney A and Nutt D (2000) Recognising and treating alcohol dependence. *Prescriber.* **5 August**: 21–30.
18 Department of Health (2000) *Attitudes to Mental Illness 2000.* Taylor Nelson Sofres. Department of Health, London.
19 Meltzer H, Gatward R, Goodman R *et al.* (2000) *The Mental Health of Children and Adolescents in Great Britain.* Office for National Statistics, London.
20 Patel A and Knapp M (1998) Costs of mental illness in England. *PSSRU Mental Health Res Rev.* **5**: 4–10.
21 NHS Executive (2000) *The NHS Plan.* NHS Executive, London.
22 Mohanna K and Chambers R (2001) *Risk Matters in Healthcare: communicating, explaining and managing risk.* Radcliffe Medical Press, Oxford.
23 Secretary of State for Health (1999) *Saving Lives: our healthier nation.* Department of Health, London.
24 Ramrakha S, Caspi A, Dickson N *et al.* (2000) Psychiatric disorders and risky sexual behaviour in young adulthood: cross-sectional study in birth cohort. *BMJ.* **321**: 263–6.
25 The Health Committee, House of Commons (2000) *Provision of NHS Mental Health Services.* The Stationery Office, London.

CHAPTER 2

Depression

How common is depression?[1-3]

Depression affects the majority of people at some time. Around 60–70% of adults will experience depression or worry of sufficient severity to influence their daily activities at some time in their lives. Episodes of depression are short-lived for most people.

Depression is one of the commonest reasons for consulting a GP. Up to 50% of people attending a general practice may have some depressive symptoms, of whom 5–10% have 'major' depression. The majority of patients with depression are treated and managed in primary care. For a GP with an average list size of 1800 patients, there will be 111 working-age adults with depression and/or anxiety that warrants treatment, and 40 older people with depression.

Episodes of 'major' depression are twice as common in women as in men. Major depression is strongly associated with adverse life and economic circumstances, such as unemployment, divorce or poor housing.

Depression is the commonest mental health problem in older people, especially in those living in nursing and residential care. Around 10–15% of older adults (aged over 65 years) have significant depressive symptoms, although major depression is rare. Women are more likely to be depressed than men.

Depressive symptoms are the fourth most important cause of disability worldwide.

The symptoms and signs of depression[1]

The symptoms are summarised in Box 2.1. Depression and anxiety often present together. Physical symptoms may be the presenting feature(s) of depression and lead to delayed or missed diagnoses of depression. One large-scale study found that doctors recognised depression in only 35% of those presenting with clinically significant depression.[2]

There are two to three times as many people with depressive symptoms as meet the criteria for major depression.[2]

Box 2.1 Criteria for 'major' depression[1]

At least five of the symptoms listed below must be present during a two-week period, of which at least one must be 'depressed mood' or 'diminished interest or pleasure':

- depressed mood
- markedly diminished interest or pleasure in normal activities
- significant weight loss or gain
- insomnia or hypersomnia
- agitated or retarded behaviour
- fatigue or loss of energy
- feelings of worthlessness or excessive guilt
- diminished ability to think or concentrate, or indecisiveness
- recurrent thoughts of death, or suicidal thoughts or actions.

The presentation of depression in older people (over 65 years of age), may be atypical, with low mood being masked. The patient may present with anxiety or memory impairment. The symptoms may be due to dementia, as depression and dementia commonly coexist.

Box 2.2 Classification of primary depression

Unipolar
- Single depressive episode
  1. mild, moderate or severe
  2. with or without somatic syndrome
  3. if severe, with or without psychotic symptoms
- Mixed anxiety and depressive disorder
- Recurrent depressive disorder
- Brief recurrent depression
- Seasonal affective disorder
- Dysthymia – depression that occurs intermittently for more than two years and does not fulfil the criteria for mild or moderate depressive episode

Bipolar
- Bipolar affective disorder
- Cyclothymia – persistent instability of mood

Box 2.2 amplifies the terms 'bipolar' and 'unipolar'. The term 'bipolar' describes depression that occurs in conjunction with manic episodes. Other depression is termed 'unipolar'.

Course of the illness[2]

About half of the people who have major depression experience a further depressive episode in the following 10 years.

Mild to moderate depression: sufferers have depressive symptoms and some functional impairment. Many individuals recover in the short term, and about 50% have recurrent symptoms.

Severe depression: sufferers have depressive symptoms together with agitation or psychomotor retardation and somatic symptoms.

Psychotic depression: sufferers have hallucinations, delusions or both, in addition to their depressive symptoms.

Box 2.3

One study of frequent attenders at general practice found that depressive symptoms were the main predictor of frequent attendance, rather than physical health problems.[4]

Suicide and self-harm

Suicide rates are higher in people with depression. It has been estimated that 40–50% of all suicides are committed by individuals with undiagnosed or inadequately treated depressive disorders.[1] Suicide accounts for 1–2% of all deaths. In young men, suicide rates have been rising sharply, whilst in older males and women they have been declining; suicide rates among men are three times higher than those among women.[5] Box 2.4 describes the plans in the National Service Framework for Mental Health for preventing suicide, and the concepts listed are generalisable throughout the UK.

Box 2.4 The approach to preventing suicide via the National Service Framework for England[6]

Local health and social care communities should prevent suicides by:

Standard 1: promoting mental health for all, working with individuals and communities.

Standard 2: delivering high-quality primary mental healthcare.

Standard 3: ensuring that anyone with a mental health problem can contact local services via the primary care team, a helpline or an Accident and Emergency department.

Standard 4: ensuring that individuals with severe and enduring mental illness have a care plan which meets their specific needs, including access to services round the clock.

Standard 5: providing safe hospital accommodation for individuals who need it.

Standard 6: enabling individuals who are caring for someone with severe mental illness to receive the support which they need to continue to care.

Standard 7: in addition to the above:
- supporting local prison staff in preventing suicides among prisoners
- ensuring that staff are competent to assess the risk of suicide among individuals at greatest risk
- developing local systems for suicide, to learn lessons and take any necessary action.

Deliberate self-harm involves intentional self-poisoning or injury. It is one of the top five causes of acute medical admissions for both women and men in the UK. Around 50–60% of patients have visited their GP in the month before the episode of self-harm.[7]

Risk factors for suicide include unemployment, low income, being single, and a history of mental illness necessitating hospital admission. High-risk groups include the mentally ill, those with a history of parasuicide, alcoholics, prisoners and certain occupational groups, such as doctors, pharmacists, farmers and vets. Methods used to commit suicide include overdose (24%), hanging (20%) and car-exhaust fumes (20%).[5]

Box 2.5

The target for the year 2010 in England is to 'reduce the death rate from suicide and undetermined injury by at least a fifth – saving 4000 lives'.[6]

Recommendations for psychiatric referral

The British Association for Psychopharmacology (BAP) has updated its evidence-based guidelines for treating depression.[8] It recommends that referral to psychiatric services is indicated:

- if there is a risk of suicide
- for psychotic symptoms
- if there is a history of a bipolar affective disorder
- if the practitioner feels insufficiently experienced to manage the patient's condition
- if two or more attempts to treat the patient's depressive disorder have failed or resulted in only a partial response.

Treatment of depressive disorders

There is evidence in the literature that several different approaches to the treatment of depressive disorders are effective, and these are outlined in Box 2.6.[2,9]

Box 2.6 Effective interventions for depression

Medication
- Tricyclic and heterocyclic antidepressants
- Monoamine oxidase inhibitors
- Selective serotonin reuptake inhibitors (SSRIs) and related drugs
- St John's Wort (in mild to moderate depression)

Psychotherapy
- Cognitive therapy (in mild to moderate depression)
- Interpersonal therapy (in mild to moderate depression)
- Problem-solving therapy (in mild to moderate depression)

Combined medication and psychotherapy

Electroconvulsive therapy

Other approaches
- Exercise (in mild to moderate depression)
- Bibliotherapy (in mild depression)

A vast array of antidepressants is available, and while there is a great deal of evidence in the literature of the effectiveness of selective serotonin reuptake inhibitor (SSRI) drugs and tricyclic antidepressants, the evidence for the effectiveness of the other neurotransmitter mechanisms outlined in Box 2.7 is limited.

Box 2.7 Other neurotransmitter agents

Selective noradrenaline reuptake inhibitor (SNRI), e.g. venlafaxine (Efexor)

Noradrenergic and specific serotonergic antidepressant (NaSSA), e.g. mirtazapine (Zispin)

Noradrenaline reuptake inhibitor (NARI), e.g. reboxetine (Edronax)

Reversible inhibitor of monoamine oxidase (RIMA), e.g. moclobemide (Manerix)

Serotonin antagonist and reuptake inhibitor (SARI), e.g. nefazodone (Dutonin)

Alpha-2 autoreceptor antagonist, e.g. mianserin (non-proprietary)

Noradrenaline and dopamine reuptake inhibitor (NDRI), e.g. bupropion (Wellbutrin)

Monoamine oxidase inhibitors (MAOIs), e.g. phenelzine (Nadil), selegiline (Deprenyl)

Other antidepressants, e.g. trazodone (Molipaxin), antihistaminergic drugs

---

Figure 2.1 shows the current guidelines for managing depression in primary care. These have been recently updated by the British Association of Psychopharmacology.[8,10,11] The guidelines will be revised as new data are published about the relative effectiveness and frequency of adverse effects of different treatments for depression. Guidelines are not strict instructions, but should help clinicians to base their management of individual patients on the evidence that exists about best practice. These guidelines emphasise the importance of choosing an antidepressant drug that best suits the individual patient.

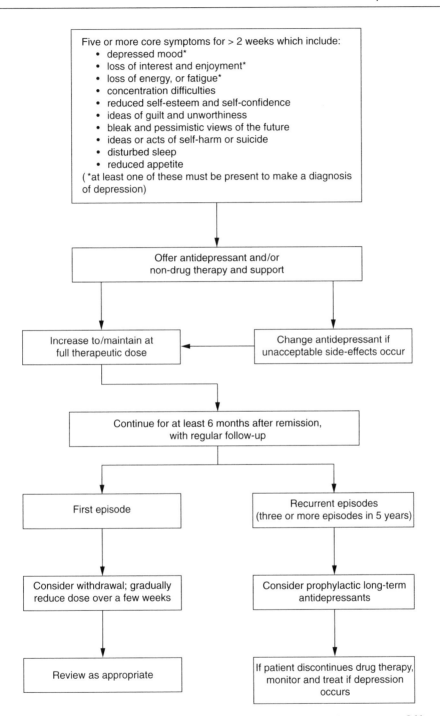

Figure 2.1: Current management guidelines for depression.[8,11]

There are several national clinical practice guidelines for depressive disorders. A recent review of such guidelines found 15 in total, of which the BAP guidelines are one.[12]

SSRIs or tricyclic antidepressants are more effective than placebo in the treatment of major and minor depressive disorders.[2] Antidepressants are also more effective than placebo in the treatment of chronic mild depressive disorders.[2]

When SSRIs are compared with tricyclic antidepressants in people with all grades of depression, there is no clinically significant difference in effectiveness.[8,9] However, SSRIs and tricyclics differ in their side-effect profiles, as shown in Table 2.1, and based on the number of people who withdrew from the clinical trials, SSRIs are better tolerated.[2] However, this difference is not large enough to justify a policy of always choosing an SSRI as a first-line treatment.[2]

Monoamine oxidase inhibitors (MAOIs) are occasionally used as second-line drugs, and must be used with caution because of the potentially serious adverse effect of a hypertensive crisis occurring without dietary limitation. Compared with tricyclic drugs, MAOIs are less effective in treating severe depressive disorders, but more effective in treating atypical depressive disorders, which are characterised by increased sleep, increased appetite, mood reactivity and rejection sensitivity.[2]

Antidepressant medication is highly effective when used properly. However, since many GPs have little training in mental health, it is not surprising that even when depression is recognised it is inadequately treated, and depressed patients may receive either no medication at all or subtherapeutic doses of medication.[13]

Selecting an antidepressant drug

There has been an explosion in the development of new antidepressant drugs in recent years, so choosing which antidepressants to use may be difficult. Table 2.1 will help to make sense of the advantages and drawbacks of using the many SSRIs and tricyclic antidepressants that are now available.

Matching the antidepressant agent to the patient

The new BAP guidelines[8] emphasise the importance of choosing the antidepressant that best suits the individual patient. Selective

Table 2.1 Advantages and drawbacks of serotonin reuptake inhibitors (SSRIs) and tricyclic drugs

Drug	Contraindication	Delay	Dependence	Overdose	Cost and efficacy (SSRI vs. tricyclic)	Adverse effects and compliance
SSRIs Fluoxetine Citalopram Sertraline Paroxetine Fluvoxamine	Sexual dysfunction, persistent insomnia, persistent agitation	Up to 2 weeks	Not addictive (although a discontinuation syndrome has been described)	Relatively safe; non-fatal	Equal efficacy to tricyclics; possibly less relapse; more expensive	Nausea, diarrhoea, headache, sleep disruption, sexual dysfunction, serotonin syndrome (rare, but may occur in combination with fenfluramine or MAOI, and may cause fever, tremor, seizures, coma and death); care is needed when SSRIs are used with other drugs metabolised by liver enzymes; well tolerated; compliance good
Tricyclic drugs Amitriptyline Imipramine Clomipramine	Suicidal ideation, heart disease, narrow-angle glaucoma	Up to 2 weeks	Not addictive (although a discontinuation syndrome has been described)	Highly toxic; convulsions, coma, sudden death	Equal efficacy to SSRIs; possibly more relapse; cheaper	Dry mouth, blurred vision, postural hypotension, ECG changes (tachyarrhythmias), constipation, urinary retention; poorly tolerated; compliance poor

serotonin reuptake inhibitors are now prescribed more frequently than tricyclic drugs. Monoamine oxidase inhibitors are prescribed very infrequently.

Although SSRIs are more expensive than tricyclic drugs, they may be more cost-effective overall, as patients are more likely to adhere to the treatment regime. The SSRIs have fewer side-effects, and are more likely to be prescribed and taken at therapeutic doses for an adequate period.

The array of clinical practice guidelines that exist for depression focus mainly on *major* depression rather than on the *mild* to *moderate* depression that is commonly seen in primary care. This does limit their applicability and relevance to those working in primary care and the types of patients who are being treated in primary as opposed to secondary care. Please see the following sections on prescribing, dependence and withdrawal for more details about dosage and maintenance treatment.

Prescribing tips

From compliance to concordance

No chapter on depression would be complete without a section on concordance, a term that highlights the GP–patient alliance in the prescribing process.[14] Research has shown that up to 8% of prescriptions for antidepressants are never dispensed.[15] Many drugs that are dispensed are not consumed. At least 25–50% of patients on antidepressant medication take irregular or insufficient doses. Improving adherence to the prescribed regime is therefore essential, and good communication between doctor and patient and more open negotiation between the two parties should help. Understanding the different philosophies of compliance and concordance may help doctors and nurses to adopt an approach that involves negotiated agreement rather than instruction.

In the past, the term 'non-compliance' was used to highlight the situation where many patients were unable or unwilling to take their medication as prescribed. However, the term 'non-compliance' portrays the unequal partnership between patients and health professionals. Implicit in the term 'compliance' is the idea that patients take orders from health professionals.

Concordance is not a synonym for compliance, as concordance is a two-way communication which recognises that the health beliefs of the patient, although different from those of the doctor, nurse or pharmacist, are no less valuable or important in deciding the best approach to the treatment of the individual. Concordance is a therapeutic partnership reached between the patient and the healthcare professional following negotiation, which respects the beliefs and wishes of the patient even if that means that they decide not to take their medicine, or to alter their treatment in some way.[14]

Patients should be counselled that it usually takes at least two weeks for them to notice any benefit from antidepressants.[9]

Box 2.8

A survey of general practice attenders determined their preferences with regard to treatment for depression. Counselling was more popular than antidepressant drugs, particularly among women, who believed that antidepressants are addictive, and/or those who had received counselling in the past.[16]

Side-effects

The range of side-effects associated with the SSRIs and the tricyclics is outlined in Table 2.1 above. The incidence of common adverse events such as nausea/vomiting, dizziness, malaise/lassitude and headache/migraine does vary between different SSRI drugs. However, a study of reports to the UK Committee on Safety of Medicines found no difference in the safety profiles of the SSRIs.[17] Adverse side-effects often cause patients to stop taking antidepressants, although for most patients the benefits of treatment far outweigh the risks. Providing adequate information and an explanation of the possible side-effects at the time of prescription, reassuring patients that the side-effects will usually subside within two or three weeks, encouraging them to continue with the medication and reassuring them that their medication could be changed if necessary can all help to increase the likelihood that they will take prescribed drugs regularly.

Selegiline or other MAOIs should not be prescribed within six weeks of discontinuing fluoxetine (because of its long half-life), or within two weeks of discontinuing paroxetine, mirtazapine or sertraline, or within one week of discontinuing citalopram, fluvoxamine or venlafaxine.

Dose

SSRI drugs can be started at the recommended maintenance dose except in the elderly, where it is wise to start with half the normal adult dose and titrate upwards as necessary to obtain clinical improvement. As most side-effects vary according to dose, it is best gradually to increase the dose until side-effects appear, and then slowly to decrease the dose until they disappear or are tolerable.[9]

Keep dosing schedules as simple as possible in order to aid concordance.

Treat major depression or dysthymia with antidepressant drugs as first-line treatment. For acute milder depression, try education, support and simple problem solving first, and monitor the patient's progress, unless there is a history of major depression, in which case start antidepressant medication. Try antidepressants if mild depression persists.[7]

Dependence and withdrawal

Reassure the patient that antidepressants are not addictive. Once an antidepressant has been taken for more than a few weeks, there should be at least a planned four-week tapering off period when they are discontinued, in order to avoid any reaction.[8] The abrupt withdrawal of SSRIs such as paroxetine and fluvoxamine, which have a short half-life, can lead to a 'discontinuation syndrome' in up to one in five patients. This is characterised by transient flu-like symptoms, including dizziness, nausea, paraesthesia, headache, tremor, palpitations, vertigo and anxiety.[2] Withdrawal reactions have been reported more frequently for paroxetine than for sertraline and fluoxetine.[2]

Suicidal ideation

Despite anecdotal reports, there is no strong evidence that fluoxetine is associated with an increased risk of suicide. A comparison of fluoxetine with a tricyclic antidepressant found that although there was no significant difference in the rate of suicidal acts between the groups, suicidal ideation was less frequent in the fluoxetine group.[2] Although the SSRIs are relatively safe in overdose, drugs should be dispensed fortnightly if suicidal ideation is suspected, until the patient is considered to be less at risk of overdose.

Continuation and maintenance treatment

Continuing treatment with antidepressant drugs for 4–6 months after recovery reduces the risk of relapse by almost half. For the elderly, this period should be extended to 12 months.[2]

Maintain long-term treatment for recurrent depressive disorder in order to prevent the recurrence of further depressive episodes. Several trials have found that maintenance treatment reduces the relapse rate in recurrent depressive disorder compared with placebo.[2] However, there is no evidence that this is so for older adults (aged over 65 years).

Consider maintenance or prophylactic treatment with antidepressant drugs for patients who have had three or more recent episodes of significant depression, or more than five episodes in total.[8]

Electroconvulsive therapy (ECT)

Electroconvulsive therapy (ECT) is effective for treating patients with acute severe depressive disorder.[2] It is a short-term treatment which may be useful when a rapid response is required. People often complain of memory impairment following ECT.

As ECT may be unacceptable to some individuals, it is best reserved for those who cannot tolerate drugs or who have not responded to other treatment where a rapid response is required in severe depression.

Specific psychological treatments

Interpersonal psychotherapy, problem-solving therapy and non-directive counselling have been found to be as effective as drugs in treating mild to moderate depression in people of all ages.[2] Another review concluded that 'there is limited evidence suggesting that, in the short term, brief counselling (generally fewer than eight sessions) delivered by practice counsellors results in better psychological symptom levels than does usual GP care in the management of a wide range of mental health problems seen in primary care. However, the clinical significance of these findings is uncertain . . . counselling may result in greater patient satisfaction, fewer mental health referrals and reduced prescribing of antidepressant drugs.'[18]

Cognitive behavioural therapy or 'thought therapy'

This was developed as a treatment for depression by Beck in 1970 in Philadelphia.[2,19] Cognitive behavioural therapy is a 'talking' therapy that is used for people suffering from depression, anxiety or eating disorders, and is adapted for those with schizophrenia in order to alleviate the symptoms of their illness. In cognitive behavioural therapy (CBT), links are made between the person's feelings and the patterns of thinking which underpin their distress. The patient is encouraged to take an active part in examining the evidence for and against distressing beliefs, challenging their habitual patterns of thinking about the belief and using reasoning and personal experience to develop rational and acceptable alternatives. Therapy may typically be carried out during 12 to 15 weekly sessions with some occasional follow-up booster sessions. It is provided by clinical psychologists, psychiatrists or community psychiatric nurses.

Cognitive therapy focuses on changing the dysfunctional beliefs and negative automatic thoughts that characterise depressive disorders. One review of published research demonstrated not only that cognitive therapy is effective, but also that it may be more effective than drug treatment in patients with mild to moderate depression.[2]

Interpersonal psychotherapy (IPT)

This is a brief, standardised treatment for depression, which usually consists of 12 to 16 weekly sessions.[2] IPT is primarily used for patients with unipolar non-psychotic depressive disorders. It is based on the assumption that psychosocial and interpersonal factors are of major significance in the development and maintenance of depression. Therefore the therapeutic techniques that are employed focus on improving the patient's interpersonal functioning within current relationships, and identifying the problems associated with the onset of the depressive episode, in order to prevent relapse. Patients are initially educated about the nature of depression and reassured that their various symptoms are part of their depression. The depressive symptoms are addressed in a similar manner to the behavioural techniques used in cognitive behavioural therapy. The therapist then moves on to address the interpersonal issues which are relevant for that individual. The main problem areas are subsequently defined and become the focus of therapy.[9]

Problem solving

This is briefer and simpler than cognitive therapy, and so may be feasible within a primary care setting.[2] It consists of three stages, namely, identifying the main problems for the patient, generating solutions and trying out the solutions.

Non-directive counselling

This was developed by Rogers in 1961 and aims to help people to express their feelings and clarify their thoughts and difficulties.[20] The therapist does not give direct advice, but suggests alternative ways of understanding and encourages people to solve their own problems.

There does not seem to be any advantage in combining drug treatment and interpersonal or cognitive therapy in mild to moderate depression. However, in severe depression, combining drug treatment and interpersonal therapy or cognitive therapy seems to be more effective than either therapy alone.[2]

St John's Wort (*Hypericum perforatum*)

St John's Wort is more effective than placebo in the treatment of mild to moderate depressive disorders, and is as effective as prescription antidepressant drugs. However, this evidence must be interpreted with caution, as the research upon which this report is based was not undertaken on fully representative groups of people using standardised preparations.[2,21]

Acupuncture

Acupuncture appears to relieve depressive symptoms. Three Chinese trials indicated that acupuncture was as effective as tricyclic anti-depressant drugs in relieving depression.[21]

Exercise

Exercise, either alone or combined with other treatments, is beneficial in mild to moderate depression.[2,21]

Bibliotherapy

Bibliotherapy consists of encouraging the patient to read 'feel-good' literature. There is limited evidence that bibliotherapy may reduce mild depressive symptoms.[2]

Older people

There are some differences between older and younger age groups. For example, suicide is more common in older people, they may be more prone to adverse effects such as falls, and as older people tend to take more medications, they are at greater risk of drug interactions.[9] However, the general principles for treating younger adults with depressive disorders apply equally well to patients over 65 years of age, and the treatments outlined above work equally well in older adults and younger ones. A systematic review is currently in progress to examine the efficacy of antidepressants in older people.[22]

Suicide[4]

No intervention has been shown to reduce suicide rates in a randomised controlled trial. Interventions that have been tried include GP educational programmes on the recognition and treatment of depressive illness, school-based suicide prevention programmes, the Samaritans, legal restrictions on drugs and firearms, safety measures at suicide hotspots and media-reporting guidelines.

Screening of high-risk groups and secondary prevention of parasuicide have not been found to reduce suicide rates.

Screening tools for depression – some examples

All of the following are screening tools; the presence of depression should be confirmed by a clinical assessment of the state of the patient's mental health.

- *Beck Depression Inventory*: this questionnaire assesses the severity of a depressive illness and measures change over time. The original version contains 21 questions, and the shorter version has 13 questions. It is suitable for patients with more severe depression and takes about three minutes to fill in.[23]
- *Edinburgh Postnatal Depression Scale*: this is a 10-item self-report questionnaire that is easy to complete. It seems to be acceptable to women, and takes only a few minutes to complete.[24]
- *General Health Questionnaire 12*: this version contains 12 questions. It is intended for use with adults aged 16 to 74 years. It takes two or three minutes to complete.[23]

- *Geriatric Depression Scale*: this questionnaire contains 15 questions, and takes about three to four minutes to complete.[23]
- *Hospital Anxiety and Depression Scale*: this questionnaire contains 14 questions. It has been devised to detect and monitor anxiety and depression.[25]

Postnatal depression

How common is it?

At least one in 10 women experience depression soon after the birth of a baby. In the UK, around 70 000 women suffer from postnatal depression each year. Most recover spontaneously within a few months, but one-third to one-half still have features of depression six months after the birth of their child, and some women continue to have chronic depressive problems. The risk factors for postnatal depression include a past history of psychiatric disorder (e.g. depression), mood disorder during the pregnancy, a poor marital relationship, lack of social support, and recent stressful life events such as bereavement or illness.[3]

Symptoms and signs of postnatal depression and course of the illness

Although postnatal depression resembles depression at other times, it differs from other depressive disorders in that it has a predictable time of onset.

Postnatal depression may have a considerable impact on the woman and her long-term relationships. It may have an adverse effect on the family as a whole, and in particular the mother–infant relationship, which may in turn affect infant cognitive and emotional development.[26] Thoughts of harming the baby are quite common. These are rarely acted upon, but they upset the depressed mother.

Treatment of postnatal depression

In comparison to depression in general, very little research has been conducted on the treatment of postnatal depression. A comprehensive review by Boath and Henshaw[27] identified only 30 treatment studies. The design of many of the studies considered in the review was deficient, so the efficacy of many of these treatment approaches has not been clearly established, and there is very little good evidence available on which to base policy or practice recommendations.

The management of postnatal depression includes support from the health visitor and others in the primary healthcare team, coupled with social support from family and friends. Until more reliable research data are published that establish their relative merits, brief psychological therapy based on non-directive counselling or cognitive behavioural therapy or antidepressant drug therapies seem to be effective treatments. Brief training programmes for healthcare professionals which include diagnostic and counselling skills have been shown to improve the care and emotional health of women postnatally, when they form part of routine care.[3]

A few mothers with severe postnatal depression need care from specialist mental health services, preferably in dedicated mother-and-baby hospital day-care and in-patient services.[3]

Reflection exercises

Exercise 2 (for practice managers and others in the primary healthcare team)

Are your records computerised with appropriate Read coding so that you can conduct audits easily and randomly select patients from various disease registers?

If your records are computerised, run an audit to check the accuracy and reliability of patients classified as having depression. For example, randomly select 20 patients from the register and look at their notes to see whether the way in which they have been diagnosed as having depression is consistent with the criteria given in Figure 2.1 earlier in this chapter. Alternatively, audit the consistency with which all of the doctors and nurses are applying Read codes as patients with depression consult them (*see* page 7).

If your records are not computerised, or if members of your practice team are not using Read codes, this might be an opportune time to agree a practice policy on these matters and make a timetabled action plan to move practice computerisation forward.

Exercise 3 (for GPs, practice nurses and practice-attached community psychiatric nurses)

Review your practice protocol for managing depression (if you have not got a practice protocol for managing depression, now is the time to write one) and what your practice team knows about diagnosis and definitions.

(i) Have you updated the protocol recently? Does it make the most of the staff and not-for-profit agencies to which you have access?

(ii) Do all members of the practice team know and understand their roles and responsibilities?
Ask them over coffee. Write down what they say and circulate it so that everyone knows what everyone else is doing. Use that material to review the skill mix in your practice team and fill the gaps whilst reducing any duplication.

(iii) Undertake an audit to check how many of those patients on antidepressant drugs have been seen in the last three months. Is the dose of antidepressants that they have been prescribed likely to be effective? Do different partners in the practice have similar prescribing patterns? If not, why not?
Take the audit results to a practice meeting. Make an action plan to remedy any deficiencies, and reaudit after you have implemented any changes to your systems and procedures.

Exercise 4 (for practice managers and GPs)

How many people have you identified as having depression in your practice population? How do the proportions compare with those in other similar practices? Ask your local public health department for any information they have about the number of patients you might expect to suffer from depression in a practice population of your size.

Compare the numbers of people who you have identified in your practice with the proportion you might expect. Do you need to redouble your efforts to identify people with depression from amongst your patients?

Exercise 5 (for GPs and practice nurses)

(i) Do you have a screening programme targeted at patients at high risk of depression in your practice?

If you do not have a screening programme, draft guidelines or a protocol to be agreed with your practice team, and start to compile a list of those patients who match the criteria for and definition of depression in your practice protocol.

If you do have a screening programme, undertake an audit of 10 residents of the local nursing home or 10 carers who are not known to have depression, and see whether they have consulted with symptoms which in retrospect might be attributable to depression.

If you do not have a manual or computerised register of carers of people with mental health problems, take 10 consecutive carers as they or their charges consult you instead.

(ii) Visit a neighbouring practice and compare the way in which you screen your patients or carers for depression with their systems and procedures. Compare your practice protocols for the management of dementia or psychoses whilst you are there. Look for gaps and refine your protocols accordingly.

> Now that you have completed these interactive reflection exercises, transfer the information about your learning needs to the empty template on pages 151–161 if you are working on your own personal development plan, or to the practice personal and professional development plan on pages 174–181 if you are working on a practice team learning plan. Don't forget to keep the evidence of your learning in your personal portfolio.

References

1 Freemantle N, Long A, Mason J et al. (1993) The treatment of depression in primary care. *Effect Health Care Bull.* **5**: 1–12.
2 Barton S (ed.) (2001) *Clinical Evidence. Issue 5.* BMJ Publishing Group, London.
3 Collier J (2000) The management of postnatal depression. *Drug Ther Bull.* **38**: 33–7.
4 Dowrick C, Bellon J and Gomez M (2000) GP frequent attendance in Liverpool and Granada: the impact of depressive symptoms. *Br J Gen Pract.* **50**: 361–5.

5 Gunnell D (1994) *The Potential for Preventing Suicide.* Health Care Evaluation Unit, Bristol.

6 National Health Service Executive (2000) *National Service Framework for Mental Health.* Department of Health, London.

7 House A, Owens D and Patchett L (1998) Deliberate self-harm. *Effect Health Care Bull.* **4(6)**: 1–12.

8 Anderson I (2000) BAP revises guidelines for antidepressant use. *Guidelines Pract.* **3**: 29–38.

9 Wilkinson G, Moore B and Moore P (2000) *Treating People with Depression.* Radcliffe Medical Press, Oxford.

10 Anderson IM, Nutt DJ and Deakin JFW (2000) Evidence-based guidelines for treating depressive disorders with antidepressants: a revision of the 1983 British Association for Psychopharmacology guidelines. *J Psychopharmacol.* **14**: 3–20.

11 Foord-Kelcey G (ed.) (2001) *Guidelines.* Medendium Group Publishing Ltd, Berkhamsted.

12 Cornwall P and Scott J (2000) Which clinical practice guidelines for depression? An overview for busy practitioners. *Br J Gen Pract.* **50**: 908–11.

13 Lepine JP, Gastpar M, Mendlewicz J and Tylee A (1997) Depression in the community: the first pan-European study of the DEPRES (Depression Research in European Society). *Int Clin Psychopharmacol.* **12**: 19–29.

14 Marinker M (ed.) (1997) *From Compliance to Concordance: achieving shared goals in medicine taking.* Royal Pharmaceutical Society in association with Merck, Sharp and Dohme, London.

15 Johnston D (1981) Depression: treatment compliance in general practice. *Acta Psychiatr Scand.* **Supplement 63**: 447–53.

16 Churchill R, Khaira M and Gretton V (2000) Treating depression in general practice: factors affecting patients' treatment preferences. *Br J Gen Pract.* **50**: 905–6.

17 Breckeneridge AM, Kendall M, Raine JM *et al.* for the Committee on Safety of Medicines (2000) Selective serotonin reuptake inhibitors (SSRIs). *Curr Prob Pharmacovigil.* **26**: 11–12.

18 Collier J (ed.) (2000) Counselling in general practice. *Drug Ther Bull.* **38**: 49–52.

19 Beck AT (1970) *Depression: causes and treatment.* University of Pennsylvania Press, Philadelphia, PA.

20 Rogers CR (1961) *On Becoming a Person.* Houghton Mifflin, Boston, MA.

21 Ernst E (ed.) (2001) *Complementary and Alternative Medicine: a desktop reference.* Harcourt Health Sciences, London.

22 Wilson K, Mottram P and Sivanthan A (1998) A review of antidepressant drug trials in the treatment of older depressed people (protocol for a Cochrane Review). In: *The Cochrane Library. Issue 4.* Update Software, Oxford.

23 Armstrong E (1997) *Primary Mental Health Care Toolkit.* Royal College of General Practitioners Unit for Mental Health Education in Primary Care, London.

24 Cox J, Holden JM and Sagovsky R (1987) Detection of postnatal depression. Development of the 10–item Edinburgh Postnatal Depression Scale. *Br J Psychiatry.* **150**: 782–6.

25 Zigmond AS and Snaith RP (1983) The Hospital Anxiety and Depression Scale. *Acta Psychiatr Scand.* **67**: 361–70.

26 Boyce PM and Stubbs JM (1994) The importance of postnatal depression. *Med J Austr.* **161**: 471–2.

27 Boath E and Henshaw C (2001) The treatment of postnatal depression: a comprehensive literature review. *J Reprod Infant Psychol.* In press.

CHAPTER 3

Generalised anxiety disorder

Anxiety is a normal response to threat or stress. Such anxiety usually improves performance in anticipating or dealing with the provoking factors. When anxiety becomes too severe, or occurs in the absence of any apparent threat, or persists, it is abnormal and the person may be diagnosed as having clinical anxiety.

Anxiety disorders include *generalised anxiety disorder*, where the anxiety is continuous, *phobic anxiety disorder*, where the anxiety is episodic, and *panic disorder*, where the anxiety is episodic without there being any consistent relationship to external stimuli.[1] The symptoms of anxiety are the same in all three conditions. This chapter will consider generalised anxiety disorder. If you want to know more about phobias or panic disorder, you can read about them elsewhere.[1,2]

What is generalised anxiety disorder (GAD)?

Generalised anxiety disorder (GAD) is defined as 'excessive worry or tension on most days for at least six months', together with the following symptoms and signs.

1 *Increased motor tension*:
  - fatiguability
  - trembling
  - restlessness
  - muscle tension.
2 *Autonomic hyperactivity*:
  - shortness of breath
  - rapid heart rate
  - dry mouth
  - cold hands
  - dizziness
but not panic attacks.

3 *Increased vigilance and scanning*:
- feeling keyed up
- increased startling
- impaired concentration.[2]

GAD is usually mild, but can be disabling if it is severe. People with anxiety disorder have a reduced quality of life and psychosocial functioning.[2] Many individuals who suffer from anxiety have a persistent fear that they have an underlying serious illness, or that someone who is close to them has such an illness.

How common is generalised anxiety disorder?

It has been estimated that one in 20 people will develop GAD at some time in their lives. It is difficult to be specific because of the frequency of short-term anxiety, stress and depressive disorders which overlap with GAD. Women appear to suffer from GAD more frequently than men.[1,3]

GAD often begins in adolescence or young adulthood, and may be lifelong. About 75% of cases persist for up to three years without treatment.[1]

It is widely held that insecure relationships in childhood predispose an individual to anxiety in later life. GADs are triggered by stressful life events.

The international classification codes (ICD-10) for anxiety disorders are listed in Box 3.1. Read codes are compatible (*see* Chapter 1, page 7).

Box 3.1 Classification of anxiety disorders[3] (ICD-10 international classification of diseases)

F40   Phobic anxiety disorder: agoraphobia, social phobia, specific phobias
F41   Other anxiety disorders
F41.0 Panic disorder
F41.1 Generalised anxiety disorder
F41.2 Mixed anxiety and depressive disorder
F42   Obsessive-compulsive disorder
F43   Reaction to severe stress and adjustment disorders
F44   Dissociative (conversion) disorders
F45   Somatoform disorders
F48   Other neurotic disorders

Exclude a physical or psychiatric cause

It is important to exclude a physical cause before diagnosing someone as suffering from anxiety. Possible physical causes with similar symptoms to those of anxiety include the following:

- thyrotoxicosis
- parathyroid disease
- hypoglycaemia, insulinoma
- phaeochromocytoma, carcinoid syndrome
- cardiac dysrhythmias
- alcohol or drug misuse/withdrawal
- drug related (e.g. bronchodilator drugs)
- excessive caffeine use.

There are also some psychiatric conditions that should be excluded from the differential diagnosis. These include panic disorder, post-traumatic stress disorder, obsessive-compulsive disorder, hypochondriasis, early dementia (where anxiety may be the first symptom) and schizophrenia (where anxiety may be linked with psychotic symptoms). All of these disorders except for panic disorder and hypochondriasis (a morbid fear of having an illness such as cancer) are covered in other chapters of the book.

Treating generalised anxiety disorder

Anxiety disorders can be treated in primary care settings by GPs, practice nurses, counsellors or health visitors, with help and support where necessary from clinical psychologists, community psychiatric nurses and psychiatrists using psychosocial and psychopharmacological treatments. Much support can be provided from the voluntary sector, by paid and volunteer workers.

There are four main interventions for the treatment of generalised anxiety for which there is evidence of effectiveness in the literature:

- psychological interventions
- certain antidepressants
- buspirone
- benzodiazepines.

The effectiveness of antipsychotic drugs or beta-blocker drugs in treating generalised anxiety disorders is unknown, as there is insufficient evidence in the literature.

Psychological treatment of anxiety: the evidence

Psychological interventions such as the following are the mainstay of treatment of GAD:

- cognitive therapy
- anxiety management training
- relaxation
- exposure therapy.

They are designed to teach the person suffering from anxiety the skills to manage the cognitive and somatic (mind and body) components of their disorder.

Psychological treatments are as effective as drug treatments, but without the risk of adverse effects from medication, although 'the efficacy of all treatments for generalised anxiety disorder is best described as modest'.[3]

Cognitive behavioural therapy

A systematic review of published research has revealed that a combination of cognitive behavioural interventions such as anxiety management training, exposure, relaxation, cognitive restructuring, relaxation training and systematic desensitisation is more effective than remaining on a waiting-list (no treatment), anxiety management training alone, relaxation training or non-directive psychotherapy.[2] Cognitive therapy was also associated with a better outcome one year later than analytical psychotherapy and anxiety management training.[2]

Problem-solving technique

This consists of three stages, namely identifying the main problems for the patient, generating solutions and trying out solutions. This approach is potentially briefer and simpler than cognitive therapy, and it may be feasible in primary care.[1] Brief counselling and structured problem-solving techniques are considered to be effective in general practice.[3]

Anxiety management training

Anxiety management training aims to help patients to control the vicious cycle of anxiety. It provides formal training in relaxation skills, which helps the patient to feel less anxious and more able to control anxiety when it does occur. This in turn allows them to generate self-reassuring instructions to promote their self-confidence, and deliberately to create anxiety-provoking thoughts and situations, which are then brought under control by replacing them with coping images and thoughts.[4]

Relaxation

Learning relaxation skills helps the patient to feel less anxious and more able to control anxiety when it does occur, and it enables them to attempt to undertake more activities. Focusing on and 'catastrophising' about anxiety symptoms serves to maintain those symptoms, so distraction is a useful short-term skill to teach the patient. If the patient feels more able to control upsetting or catastrophic thoughts, they will be more likely to control the vicious cycle of anxiety. Such techniques are usually presented and practised in anxiety management groups, but can be quickly outlined by the GP or practice nurse to patients who appear to be sufficiently articulate and motivated to develop the skills necessary to help themselves.

Applied relaxation is a technique that involves imagining relaxing situations in order to produce muscular and mental relaxation.

Exposure therapy

Exposure therapy has been shown to be very useful in treating patients with phobias, panic disorder or compulsive rituals. Various anxiety management strategies are taught and practised until the person is competent in their use, prior to exposure to the usual stimuli. Then, using a series of planned and systematic exposure exercises, the patient is encouraged to identify and stay in contact with a stimulus or frightening situation which they have previously been avoiding, for up to 1–2 hours per day in order to 'test out' their fears. During exposure, maladaptive beliefs are challenged, and the previous fears gradually disappear as the person becomes used to the original stimuli and realises that actually nothing 'bad' occurs as a result.[4]

Eye movement desensitisation and reprocessing (EMDR)

This is a new treatment of unproven efficacy.[1,4] Treatment basically consists of the patient performing repetitive rapid eye movements while imagining the traumatic event in their 'mind's eye'. The person being treated is asked to follow the therapist's finger as it moves from side to side. EMDR usually requires an average of four sessions. Treatment is focused on visual memories of the most traumatic features of the event, salient personal meanings related to the event and associated physical sensations.

Box 3.2 An integrated counselling service[5]

Leigh Primary Care Group has set up an integrated counselling service for everyone living in its constituency. Leigh has a population with higher than average mental health needs. The primary care group is establishing a system in which there is a named counsellor in place in each practice. They are developing an integrated pathway of care to provide a service based on need. The service provides staff with support and education through multidisciplinary team training. This includes practice nurses, health visitors, district nurses and midwives, as well as GPs and community psychiatric nurses.

The community psychiatric nurses and psychologists employed by the trust work closely with the primary care counsellors to develop a seamless service of referrals. There are close links with other counsellors from the Citizens' Advice Bureau, Relate and the local Family Churches Association.

A lead counsellor from the scheme co-ordinates the data collection, arranges inter-agency working, ensures that protocols and standards are followed, and develops training and education in line with continuing professional development of the various disciplines. The cost of counselling services works out at approximately £13.50 per hour.

Psychopharmacological interventions: the evidence

Medication is a secondary treatment in the management of GAD. Although pharmacological interventions by themselves are unlikely to be of enduring benefit, they are useful if significant symptoms of anxiety persist despite psychological intervention, or if symptoms of depression are also present.[4]

There is increasing evidence that combining psychological treatments with medication reduces the rate of relapse after stopping pharmacological medication.[4] This clearly has important implications not only for long-term costs (reducing future consultations, etc.), but also in promising a much more positive outlook for the individual in terms of future morbidity (and indeed mortality, which has been shown to be increased in chronic anxiety states).

The evidence for the effectiveness of pharmacological interventions in the treatment of GAD is outlined below.

Benzodiazepines[2,4]

Several studies have suggested that benzodiazepines are no more effective than simple counselling, psychotherapy or anxiety management in over 50% of those individuals with anxiety who are normally considered to be suitable candidates for anxiolytic drugs. The remainder probably need psychotropic drugs as well as non-drug treatments.

Benzodiazepines are an effective and rapid treatment for GAD. However, they should be avoided if possible because of their adverse effects, namely cognitive impairment of attention, concentration and short-term memory. They carry an increased risk of industrial and road-traffic accidents. One systematic review of road-traffic accidents found that benzodiazepine use was a factor in 1–65% (usually 5–10%) of road-traffic accidents.

Benzodiazepines do cause dizziness, drowsiness and sedation, which can also interfere with concomitant psychotherapy. There is a high risk of substance abuse and dependence with benzodiazepines. Up to one in five users become long-term users, and true dependence occurs in about one-third of users. Thus benzodiazepines should rarely be prescribed for more than a few days, or up to two weeks for short-term treatment for overwhelming anxiety (e.g. arising as a result of a disaster), or up to four weeks on an as-required basis to treat anxiety exacerbation that sometimes occurs with antidepressant treatment of panic disorder.[6] Rebound anxiety has been reported on withdrawal, and therefore even in short-term use the dose should be reduced and tapered off to minimise rebound effects.

> **Box 3.3**
>
> 'Some patients – especially those with chronic anxiety, a tendency to self-treat with alcohol, and a long history of benzodiazepine use – are difficult to manage except with benzodiazepines. When benzodiazepines are used, those with a slower onset of action (not the same as half-life), such as oxazepam, may cause less dependence and withdrawal symptoms than diazepam or lorazepam'.[3]

There is no significant difference between sustained-release alprazolam and bromazepam. There is no difference in effectiveness between benzodiazepines and buspirone.

Benzodiazepines should be avoided late in pregnancy and while breastfeeding. Their use in late pregnancy has been associated with neonatal hypotonia and withdrawal syndrome. Benzodiazepines are secreted in breast milk, and there have been reports of sedation and hypothermia in infants.

For current dosing schedules, refer to the *British National Formulary*.[6]

Buspirone[2]

Buspirone is effective in treating GAD. However, in contrast to benzodiazepines, it may take up to two weeks before an effect is observed, but this delay is counterbalanced by the fact that it has fewer adverse effects. Buspirone is no more or less effective in treating GAD than antidepressants or benzodiazepines.

Adverse effects include nausea, dizziness and headache, and very rarely buspirone may cause palpitations, chest pain, dry mouth, fatigue and sweating. There are no reports of dependency or adverse effects on pregnancy or breastfeeding.

Previous exposure to benzodiazepines reduces the response to buspirone.

Antidepressant drugs[2]

The tricyclic antidepressants that have marked serotonergic activity, such as clomipramine, amitriptyline and imipramine, have all been shown to be effective in treating people suffering from anxiety, especially those with marked depressive symptoms.

Paroxetine (a selective serotonin reuptake inhibitor or SSRI), imipramine (a tricyclic), trazodone (a sedative antidepressant) and venlafaxine (a selective noradrenaline reuptake inhibitor or SNRI) are all effective in controlling the symptoms of anxiety, even in patients with no depressive symptoms. Paroxetine and imipramine have been found to be more effective than a benzodiazepine in improving anxiety scores after 8 weeks.

Venlafaxine and buspirone do not differ significantly in their effectiveness when taken over a period of 8 weeks. Monoamine oxidase inhibitors (MAOIs) have also been used to treat anxiety and were found to be effective, but they are best used under specialist supervision.[4]

The side-effects of antidepressants are described in Table 2.1. There is a significant risk of sedation, confusion and falls with these drugs, and a high risk of arrhythmias in the event of overdose with tricyclic drugs. Older people taking antidepressants are at particular risk of falls and hip fracture.

Treatment of GAD often requires higher doses of antidepressants than are used in depression, as well as a longer duration of treatment.[7] A maintenance dose should be prescribed for 6–12 months in order to prevent relapse, and should only be stopped once the patient has been free of symptoms for 3 months.

Antipsychotic drugs[2]

Trifluoperazine is more effective than placebo in treating GAD. However, this drug is associated with the serious adverse effects of sedation, acute dystonias, akathisia, parkinsonism and tardive dyskinesia.

Beta-blocker drugs[2]

There is no evidence that beta-blockers are useful in the long-term treatment of GAD – they have not been adequately evaluated for this purpose.[1,4]

Box 3.4

'Despite propranolol being widely used to treat anxiety (but interestingly only in the UK), this and other beta-blockers are only effective for the treatment of specific symptoms (e.g. tremor and sweating that are particularly problematic in performance anxiety seen in musicians, etc.) . . . Beta-blockers are of no proven benefit in any other type of anxiety and do have risks associated with their use (e.g. in patients with asthma or heart problems).'[7]

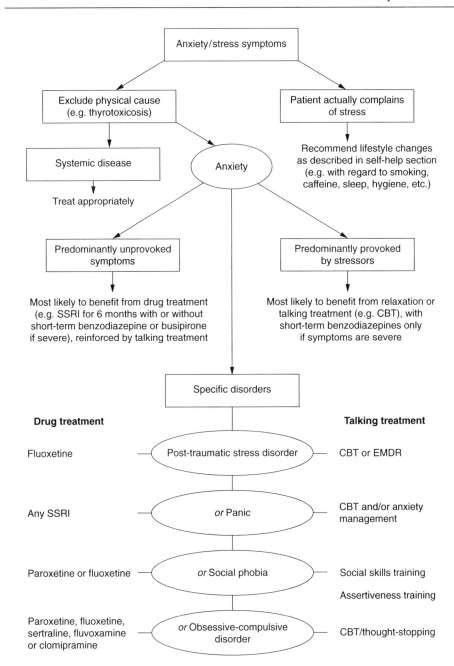

Figure 3.1: The anxiety treatment tree, an algorithm for the management of anxiety disorders[4,8] (reproduced with permission from Wilkinson G, Moore B and Moore P (2000) *Treating People with Anxiety and Stress.* Radcliffe Medical Press, Oxford).

SSRI, selective serotonin reuptake inhibitor; CBT, cognitive behavioural therapy; EMDR, eye movement desensitisation retraining.

Treatment of refractory anxiety

If a patient fails to respond to any of the conventional drug treatments outlined above, review the diagnosis. Physical causes of symptoms should be reconsidered before commencing a new drug regime. If anxiety symptoms persist or the patient deteriorates despite active treatment, refer him or her to a specialist.

Matching agent to patient

The 'Anxiety Decision Tree' shown in Figure 3.1 is a simple-to-follow algorithm for the management of patients who present with anxiety symptoms. It is based on research findings, but is not intended to be prescriptive. As always, the clinician and patient should arrive at the treatment plan that is most suitable for the individual patient. A good therapeutic alliance between patient and therapist remains the most valuable component of treatment.

Reflection exercises

Exercise 6 (for practice teams)

Undertake a significant event audit around a serious adverse condition that has occurred recently in a patient with a mental health problem – for instance, someone suffering from generalised anxiety who has been treated with benzodiazepines by the practice and subsequently had a road accident that left him with a fractured pelvis. Look at the circumstances leading up to the event.

Discuss the case as a practice team, looking to see whether you could have used alternative interventions to benzodiazepines at any time before the serious event occurred. Could your management have been different?

Exercise 7 (for GPs and practice nurses)

Undertake an audit of all those patients with persistent anxiety disorders to see whether you have been giving them balanced advice about their lifestyles and not been distracted by their anxiety disorders and frequent and demanding consulting behaviour.

(i) Have you recorded current smoking status in the last year?

(ii) Do you know which interventions for smoking cessation are most likely to be successful and for which patients the different interventions are warranted?

(iii) Have you checked each patient's blood pressure in the last five years? If so, were the results in the recommended ranges ($< 140/80$ mmHg)?

(iv) Have you calculated their body mass index and advised them about losing weight if they are overweight or obese?

(v) Have you enquired about how much exercise or other physical activity they take, and encouraged them to keep active?

Exercise 8 (for GPs and practice nurses)

Having read through the material in this chapter, do you have a good understanding of the effectiveness of the various interventions described? Or do you need to read and study more? You could look up the references cited here.

Now that you have completed these interactive reflection exercises, transfer the information about your learning needs to the relevant section in the empty template on pages 151–161 if you are working on your own personal development plan, or to the practice personal and professional development plan on pages 174–181 if you are working on a practice team learning plan. Don't forget to keep the evidence of your learning in your personal portfolio.

References

1 Barton S (2001) *Clinical Evidence. Issue 5.* BMJ Publishing Group, London.
2 Weatherall DJ, Ledingham JG and Warrell DA (1996) *Oxford Textbook of Medicine* (3e). Oxford Medical Publications, New York.
3 Hale AS (1997) Anxiety. ABC of mental health. *BMJ.* **314**: 1886–9.
4 Wilkinson G, Moore B and Moore P (2000) *Treating People with Anxiety and Stress.* Radcliffe Medical Press, Oxford.

5 Hilton J (2000) Counselling service aims to take the weight off our GPs. *Primary Care Report.* **May**: 31–4.

6 Mehta DK (2000) *British National Formulary.* September 2000. British Medical Association and the Royal Pharmaceutical Society, London.

7 Bell C (2000) Anxiety management. *Prescriber.* **19 June**: 46–8.

8 den Boer (1999) *Literature Review.* Presented at European Neuroscience Conference, 18–20 March, Madrid.

CHAPTER 4

Obsessive-compulsive disorder

What is obsessive-compulsive disorder?

Obsessive-compulsive disorder (OCD) is characterised by 'obsessions, compulsions, or both, that cause significant personal distress or social dysfunction, and that are not caused by drugs or physical disorder'.[1] Thoughts intrude repeatedly and persistently into a person's consciousness, and are recognised by that person as being irrational and pointless.[2] The intrusive thoughts are usually associated with repetitive behaviours or rituals. The anxiety and fear that the person experiences relate to the consequences of the thoughts rather than to the objects of the thoughts themselves.

Obsessions and compulsions have been defined as follows: 'Obsessions are recurrent and persistent ideas, images or impulses that cause pronounced anxiety and which the person (suffering from OCD) perceives to be self-produced. Compulsions are intentional repetitive behaviours or mental acts performed in response to obsessions or according to certain rules and are aimed at reducing distress or preventing certain imagined dreaded events.'[1]

People suffering from OCD often feel ashamed of their disorder and try to conceal their behaviour. The disorder causes real distress to the sufferer and their families. The sufferer usually tries to resist the compulsion they feel to perform their rituals, but without success.

A common theme is an obsession about spreading disease by touching objects and contaminating them, thereby leading to compulsive handwashing and cleansing of the environment. Some obsessional thoughts involve the affected person imagining him- or herself performing dangerous or embarrassing activities.

About two-thirds of cases of those experiencing OCD for the first time resolve within a year. The rest may continue for many years in intermittent or continuous forms, remitting and relapsing or persisting.[2]

Who suffers from obsessive-compulsive disorder?

Obsessional disorders may be triggered by increased stress but then persist after the stress has apparently resolved.

The research evidence is inconclusive as to whether there is a genetic cause.[2,3] Behavioural, cognitive, genetic and neurobiological factors have all been implicated.[1]

How common is it?

One study in the UK found the prevalence of OCD to be 1% in men (1 in 100 men) and 1.5% (3 in 200) in women. Other research on non-UK populations has found higher prevalence rates.[1,3]

Around 20% of people with depression have a marked obsessive-compulsive component to their disorder, and 80% of individuals who suffer from anorexia nervosa display obsessive-compulsive traits.[3]

Treatment – the evidence

There is evidence that OCD can be effectively treated by the following:[1]

- antidepressant drugs (*see* Table 4.1)
- behavioural therapy
- cognitive therapy
- drug treatment together with behavioural therapy.

When the obsessive-compulsive disorder is mild and of recent onset, drug treatment should not be instituted. The treatment should be supportive, with the patient being encouraged to resist performing rituals.[2]

Antidepressant treatment

The antidepressant drugs currently licensed for the treatment of OCD and the suggested prescribing regimens are shown in Table 4.1.

Table 4.1 Treatment of obsessive-compulsive disorder with anti-depressant drugs[3]

Antidepressant	Class	Recommended regimen
Sertraline	SSRI	50 mg daily, increasing gradually, if necessary, to a maximum of 200 mg per day
Fluoxetine	SSRI	20 mg daily, increasing gradually, if necessary, to a maximum of 60 mg per day
Paroxetine	SSRI	20 mg daily, increasing gradually, if necessary, to a maximum of 60 mg per day
Fluvoxamine	SSRI	100 mg daily, increasing gradually, if necessary, to a maximum of 300 mg per day
Clomipramine	Tricyclic	10 mg daily, increasing gradually, if necessary, to a maximum of 250 mg per day

All of the antidepressants listed in Table 4.1 have been shown to be more effective than placebo in treating OCD.[1] There are no differences in efficacy between the selective serotonin reuptake inhibitors (SSRIs). There is some limited evidence that sertraline (an SSRI) is more effective at reducing the symptoms of OCD than clomipramine and desipramine (tricyclic drugs).[1] However, there is no evidence of differences in efficacy between clomipramine (a tricyclic) and fluoxetine or fluvoxamine (SSRIs).[1]

Clomipramine has more adverse side-effects than the SSRIs (*see* Table 2.1 in Chapter 2 for the adverse effects of antidepressant drugs). However, clomipramine might be tried if there is a poor response to full doses of SSRIs.[3]

Duration and discontinuation of treatment

Reliable research suggests that a minimum period of 10–12 weeks is required to assess treatment efficacy.[1] Although the response to medication may be good, it may not last. One follow-up study found that most patients relapsed within 7 weeks of stopping drug treatment. Therefore it is important to encourage patients to take a maintenance dose for 3–6 months after the symptoms have remitted.[1]

However, in some cases drug treatment alone may not work, or may not be sufficient to ensure a sustained recovery. In such cases, where services allow, psychological approaches such as behavioural therapy and cognitive therapy, or combined drug and psychological intervention therapy, may provide long-term solutions.

Psychological treatments for OCD: the evidence

Behavioural therapy

This is the traditional approach to the treatment of OCD. It consists of exposing the patient to distressing thoughts or anxiety-provoking stimuli and preventing them from making a response. This encourages the patient to block any ritualistic performances, compulsive thoughts or behaviours.

One research study showed that improvement was maintained for up to two years after behavioural therapy, but that some patients required additional behavioural therapy.[1]

Cognitive therapy

This approach focuses on changing distorted beliefs and thoughts. It aims to modify and correct thoughts, such as erroneous beliefs about personal responsibility or an exaggerated sense of harm. The patient is encouraged to relate their specific fears during behavioural tests. Logical reasoning and hypothesis testing are used to question negative automatic thoughts. The patient is then encouraged to reassess and recognise alternative interpretations of events that may be equally valid (compared to the previous negative thoughts) and lead to more helpful and positive responses.

Box 4.1

Cognitive behavioural therapy is founded on the concept that 'events do not cause distress; rather it is our interpretations of these events that bring about our emotional reactions and behaviours'. The process of interpreting events is analysed at three levels of thinking: *core beliefs*, from which the individual develops certain *assumptions and rules* that allow him or her to function (schemata), and *negative automatic thinking*.[4]

If behavioural or cognitive therapy is chosen, this is best administered by experienced therapists, as the time required to apply this approach successfully (e.g. 50 minutes per session) is far greater than the time that most primary healthcare professionals have available.

Box 4.2 An integrated model for the delivery of mental healthcare across the interface of primary and secondary care[5]

The key components of this 'beacon site' are as follows:

- a 'whole-system' approach for delivering primary and secondary care across the interface
- a training system for practice nurses, primary care nurses and GPs
- a training course in cognitive behavioural therapy for psychosis and family interventions to improve the delivery of care for patients with serious mental illness
- the role of the community psychiatric nurse (CPN) trained in psychosocial intervention techniques is aligned with primary care. The CPN provides clinical supervision for nurses and doctors in primary care
- an integrated care programme approach (CPA) and risk assessment tool with local social services departments
- primary care services are encouraged to detect and refer psychoses at an early stage
- the development of a network in primary care includes the voluntary sector to detect early psychosis and help patients to engage with services
- a resource centre for mental health training materials.

Contact: Medical Adviser, Bedfordshire and Luton Community Trust. Tel: 01582 708999.

Comparison of pharmacological and psychological treatments

There is no significant difference in efficacy between cognitive therapy and behavioural therapy, but behavioural therapy is more effective in reducing symptoms than is relaxation.[1] However, there is evidence that behavioural therapy together with fluvoxamine is more effective than behavioural therapy alone,[1] although there is no evidence that cognitive therapy together with fluvoxamine is better than cognitive therapy alone.

Given the evidence for combined drug and behavioural therapy approaches, GPs should work closely with therapists to ensure an effective long-term cure.[3]

Reflection exercise

Exercise 9 (for GPs)

Review the extent to which you are detecting obsessive-compulsive disorder and the extent to which you are successful in helping patients with obsessive-compulsive disorder to gain control over their symptoms.

(i) Ask the next 20 consecutive patients who consult you with depression whether they have any obsessional or compulsive behaviour.
It may be that they have not volunteered these symptoms before, and direct questioning may elicit new information about their illness.

(ii) Review the case notes of any patients identified as having obsessive-compulsive disorder and look at what treatment they have been given – pharmacological or psychological. How does it compare with the best practice described in this chapter?
If you have classified patients by Read coding (*see* page 7) and can identify 10 patients with OCD, then audit those case notes. If you do not have such a computerised system, see how many patients you can recall and ask other practice colleagues which patients they can remember. Reviewing 10 patients' notes should give you an idea of how well you are doing as an individual or as a practice.

(iii) What do you and your team need to learn from this exercise and what re-organisation of the practice do you need to make? Do you know where to refer patients for behavioural or cognitive therapy? Do you need to undertake further reading about OCD and the range of anxiety disorders? Do you need more systematic data recording about patients' conditions on computer?
Draw up your action plan accordingly – including service development and learning activities.

> Now that you have completed this interactive reflection exercise, transfer the information about your learning needs to the relevant section in the empty template on pages 151–161 if you are working on your own personal development plan, or to the practice personal and professional development plan on pages 174–181 if you are working on a practice team learning plan. Don't forget to keep the evidence of your learning in your personal portfolio.

References

1 Barton S (2001) *Clinical Evidence. Issue 5.* BMJ Publishing Group, London.
2 Weatherall DJ, Ledingham JG and Warrell DA (1996) *Oxford Textbook of Medicine* (3e). Oxford Medical Publications, New York.
3 Wilkinson G, Moore B and Moore P (2000) *Treating People with Anxiety and Stress.* Radcliffe Medical Press, Oxford.
4 Enright S (2000) Cognitive therapy: a practical guide. *Practitioner.* **244**: 426–35.
5 NHS Beacon Services (2000) *NHS Beacon Learning Handbook 2000/2001.* Volume 1. NHS Beacon Services, Petersfield.

CHAPTER 5

Stress

What is stress?

Stress is very difficult to define as it is such a vague word and everyone interprets it differently. Stress is equivalent to a person's perception of the pressure upon them, or the 'three-way relationship between demands on a person, that person's feelings about those demands and their ability to cope with those demands'.[1] Stress may result either from stressful events themselves or from the person's perception of them. A particular event or task can be very stressful for someone one day but not on another – all depending on how they are feeling and what other pressures are being exerted on them.

In general, stress occurs in situations where demands are high, control over the demands is limited, and too little is available in the form of support or help.

Different occupations have their own stresses intrinsic to the nature of the job – the pressure to sell and remain financially solvent in business, or the stress from caring for ill people with limited resources in the health professions. Job insecurity is a potent source of stress. A person's role in their employing organisation may be stressful, too – for instance, taking responsibility for other people, uncertainty about what is required, or being under-skilled for the post's responsibilities.[2,3]

Box 5.1 Comparison of the extent of stress felt by managers and health professionals[4]

A study of NHS staff in 1998 compared the results with those from research into workers from other organisations. The results showed that the percentage of those scoring as *stressed* according to the General Health Questionnaire-12 (GHQ-12) was as follows:

- NHS managers   33%
- manufacturing managers   23%
- nurses   28%
- professions allied to medicine   27%
- doctors (employed by trusts)   25%
- administrative staff   24%
- GPs (other studies[5])   30–48%.

Disturbing life events

In addition to stress from everyday life at work and home, changes in lifestyle can create additional stress.[6] These may concern relationships (e.g. marriage, divorce, bereavement, births, etc.) or changes in circumstances (e.g. moving house, switching jobs, retirement). The level of stress that a particular event incurs depends on how the person involved views that event and how well they are able to absorb or manage stress. Several changes in lifestyle are additive.

What health professionals find stressful

The types of factors that GPs and other health professionals most commonly describe as causing them to feel stressed from their work[2,7–9] include the following:

- patients' inappropriate expectations
- interruptions
- practice administration
- the conflict at the work–home interface between career and family
- interference with social life
- dealing with death and dying
- making mistakes
- fear of litigation
- work/demand overload.

Is stress bad?

The answer to this question depends on how much stress a person is under, for how long it is applied, and whether the person feels powerless to cope with the stress or is able to overcome it. A moderate amount of stress is necessary to perform well at work, to function in general and to maintain a zest for life. Zero stress may lead to boredom, whereas too much stress over too long a period will render a person indecisive, exhausted or burnt out.

It is important to distinguish between an occasional event or task that creates the highest levels of stress, and those situations that cause the most frequent reports of stress. A steady relentless 'drip, drip, drip' of stress-provoking situations may be just as likely to result in a stressed person as a single crisis event with monumental stress attached.

Box 5.2

'Stress is the spice of life' – Hans Selye

Stress may be the spice of life, but it is also the scourge of the twenty-first century.

Stress affects the whole of today's society. It is estimated that around 80 million working days are lost each year in the UK due to stress-related disorders, at a cost of £3.7 billion. Up to 60% of absenteeism is thought to be due to mental or emotional problems. Around 10% of the work-force in the UK have been estimated to experience emotional and physical ill health related to occupational stress, and about 7% of GP consultations involve patients with work-related stress.[3,10]

Effects of stress

Stress at work does not happen in a 'vacuum'. Pressures and problems at home often influence how someone feels and performs at work, and vice versa – the effects of stress at work are often taken home and unfairly dumped there.

Stress affects everyone at one time or another. It often goes undetected or unacknowledged by the sufferer him- or herself. Sufferers may have been warned by others to 'slow down', and may have delighted in ignoring such advice and pushing themselves on regardless.

Box 5.3 Stressful life events, social support and mortality in men born in 1933[11]

A survey of 752 Swedish men aged 50 years found that life events were significantly associated with mortality. Of the men who had experienced three or more life events during the previous year after completing a baseline assessment, 10.9% had died during the subsequent seven years, compared with 3.3% of those men who had experienced no life events. The link between multiple life events and death was demonstrated even after smoking, occupational class and the level of social support were taken into account. Many of the deaths were alcohol related and occurred in men with low levels of emotional support. The life events that were reported included serious illness or death in the family, divorce or separation, being forced to move house or change job, redundancy, feelings of insecurity at work, serious financial problems and being legally prosecuted.

Men who were receiving adequate emotional support from a partner, family and friends appeared to be protected from the effects of stress due to various life events. Social support appears to moderate the impact of stress through a buffering effect.

Stress is a very real problem that leads not only to a range of psychological consequences such as anxiety and depression, but also to a range of physiological consequences such as hypertension, an increased risk of cancer and coronary heart disease, and low-birth-weight infants.[12]

Physical, mental, emotional and behavioural symptoms – individuals

Different people experience different proportions and mixes of physical, mental, emotional and behavioural symptoms. The types of symptoms that might occur are listed in Table 5.1.[2,3,7,8]

Stress and performance

There is a common misconception by employers and their work-force that there is a linear relationship between the extent of demands applied to individuals and their performance at work. Instead, there is an optimum level of demand at which the individual is decisive,

Table 5.1 Symptoms and signs of stress

Behavioural symptoms and signs	Emotional/mental symptoms and signs	Physical symptoms and signs
Loss of confidence	Anxiety	Nausea/indigestion
Avoiding paperwork	Palpitations	Headaches
Procrastinating, indecisive	Feeling burdened	Migraines
Shunting work away	Insomnia	Skin disorders
Working all weekends	Panic/	Chest pains
Under-performing	hyperventilation	General aches and
Less efficient	Reduced or increased	pains
Late for work	appetite	Raised blood pressure
Longer working hours but	Feeling tired/drained	Trembling
less done	Feeling jumpy/	Sweating
Breakdown of relationships	irritable	Cold hands and feet
Argumentative, irritable	Difficulty in	Weakness
Accident prone	concentrating	Shortness of breath
Loss of interest in sex	Depression	Constant tiredness
Overeating	Cynicism	
Withdrawal from	Loss of confidence	
relationships	Lack of self-esteem	
Excessive use of alcohol,	Feeling helpless	
tobacco or caffeine	Loss of sense of	
Unusual absences	humour	
Poor judgement	Feeling guilty	

creative, and working efficiently and effectively. After this point, if a sensible level of demand is exceeded, performance tails off and the individual becomes less effective, less decisive, etc., and eventually they become exhausted and burnt out. Figure 5.1 illustrates this sequence of events and the fantasy line.[2]

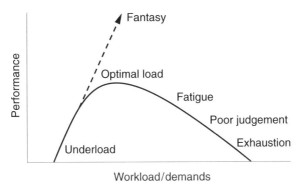

Figure 5.1: Stress performance curve.

Effects of stress in the workplace

There are profound effects on an organisation in which many of the work-force are suffering from stress. The resulting physical and mental symptoms spill over to affect all aspects of performance at work. Detrimental effects on relationships with others at work can result, including the following:

- poor team spirit/work
- breakdown in communication
- too little time for each other, so no deep bonds of friendship or regard are formed
- too little support for each other
- others feel stressed when they are in the company of the stressed person.

The outcomes of such stress for the working of an organisation may include inefficiency and many or all of the following (to a greater or lesser extent):

- less effective work
- reduced productivity
- lack of creativity
- an increase in the number of errors
- relationship problems with clients, customers, superiors, juniors and staff
- poor or bad decision making
- job dissatisfaction
- poor timekeeping
- disloyalty
- increased sick leave
- increased complaints
- high staff turnover/premature retirement
- absenteeism
- accidents
- thefts
- organisational breakdown.

Effects of stress on a person's home life

The effects of stress can damage people's relationships with their families and friends, just as stress at work can adversely affect their

relationships with work colleagues. The types of effects of stress due to life outside work that might result include the following:

1 family and partner bonds deteriorate if the stressed person is preoccupied with his or her own feelings and appears to be disinterested in others
2 one problem creates another
3 there is a lack of support and cohesion
4 children/spouses feel that they are unimportant compared to the stressed person's work, if the stress is emanating from work
5 breakdown of the family unit
6 the adverse effects of behavioural symptoms (*see* Table 5.1 above) make the individual's situation worse and strain personal relationships further.

Treatment and management of stress

Although a variety of physiological, psychological and pharmacological interventions have been used for stress reduction, the methodological limitations of much of the underlying research mean that there is little firm evidence of the effectiveness of these approaches.[13] A comprehensive search of the literature revealed only one systematic review of the treatment of stress[14] and one meta-analysis.[15]

Despite the lack of concrete research evidence, it is important that stress is managed effectively in primary care. Much work has been carried out on the treatment and management of stress in healthcare professionals,[2,7-9,16] and many of these lessons could be transferred to patients in the primary care setting.

Drug treatment of stress: the evidence

Most cases of stress are self-limiting and will respond adequately to adaptation, problem solving or changing the environment. However, drug treatment may be necessary in cases of severe stress, or where drug and alcohol abuse are complicating factors. A good guiding principle is to treat stress according to the predominant symptoms, and suggested regimens are summarised in Table 5.2 (modified from Wilkinson *et al.*[17]).

Table 5.2 Pharmacological treatment of stress

Symptoms	Medication	Regimen
Acute stress reaction or adjustment disorder (marked agitation)	Lorazepam*	1 mg orally as required up to a maximum of 4 mg
	Diazepam*	2–5 mg orally as required up to 15 mg daily for 1 or 2 days only
Depression with anxiety	SSRI	Prescribe according to *British National Formulary* recommendations, and review monthly
Insomnia	Zolpidem†	5–10 mg orally at night
	Zopiclone†	3.75–7.5 mg orally at night
Post-traumatic stress disorder	SSRI (e.g. paroxetine or fluoxetine)	Prescribe according to *British National Formulary* recommendations (e.g. paroxetine 20–40 mg or fluoxetine 20–40 mg, each daily for 6 months)

* Warning: high potential for dependence.
† Warning: modest potential for dependence.

Although medication may be useful for the short-term treatment of stress, the adverse effects of many of these drugs (as outlined in other chapters in this book), combined with the fact that drugs treat only the symptoms and not the root of the problem, mean that medication should not be regarded as a long-term cure.

Psychological treatment of stress: the evidence

Stress often occurs when an individual's perception of the demands of a situation does not match their perceived ability to meet those demands.[1] The crucial factor is not their actual ability to meet the demands, but their perceived ability, and for this reason a range of psychological and behavioural strategies have been used to treat stress.

Autogenic training

This involves a system of very specific autosuggestive formulas that are repeated in a specific pattern, and formularised resolutions that are repeated up to 30 times. Developed by Schultz in 1932, autogenic training draws heavily on hypnosis and yoga. Almost anyone can learn autogenic training by reading a self-help book, and the technique can be mastered within just a few weeks. However, the evidence of the efficacy of autogenic training is very limited, and one systematic review of eight controlled trials of autogenic training as a means of reducing stress and anxiety reached no firm conclusion about its effectiveness as a result of the methodological flaws in the trials.[14]

Stress inoculation training (SIT)[18,19]

This is an individually tailored form of cognitive behavioural therapy that aims to help individuals to cope with stressful events, and to use existing coping strategies to 'inoculate' clients against ongoing stressors. Clients are informed about the impact and nature of stress and how they may inadvertently be exacerbating their levels of stress. Clients are encouraged to:

- view stressors as problems to be solved
- identify which aspects of their situation are potentially changeable and which are not
- break down stressors into specific short-term, intermediate and long-term coping goals.

Stress inoculation training is effective in reducing performance anxiety and state anxiety, and in enhancing performance under stress.[15] It is also used to treat post-traumatic stress disorder.[17]

Cognitive behavioural therapy (CBT)

This focuses on modifying cognitive defences, cognitive reappraisal and developing adaptive behavioural responses. Although there have been a number of research studies evaluating CBT as a method of stress management, methodological problems with these studies, such as the lack of an appropriate control group, mean that there is little firm evidence to support the effectiveness of CBT.[17]

Exercise

This addresses the effects of stress mediated through physiological responses to cause physical complications, such as hypertension, increased risk of cancer, and coronary heart disease.[12] Active behavioural strategies such as exercise have been found to reduce catecholamine levels in stressed individuals, and are readily accepted by patients as a means of 'releasing tension'. However, there is no reliable research evidence in the form of systematic reviews of the effectiveness of such an approach.

Stress management training (SMT)

This has been used to treat workplace stress, and is usually offered to groups of staff rather than to individuals. Such training usually includes an educational component, training in relaxation, goal setting and evaluation, and practical skills such as time management. Participants are encouraged to develop coping behaviours that include changing their environment as well as themselves.[2,6,7,9] However, there is no standard SMT programme manual, and as each programme is unique it is impossible to replicate in future evaluative studies, generalise to other groups or assess which are the key components of the programme.

There are no systematic reviews of SMT, and therefore little evidence for the effectiveness of these programmes. However, despite the methodological flaws, evaluations of SMT programmes have resulted in apparent improvements in self-reported psychological and stress-related symptoms, although these are generally short-lived.[9]

Post-traumatic stress disorder[17]

Post-traumatic stress disorder (PTSD) is a 'delayed or protracted response to a stressful event or trauma to a degree sufficiently threatening or catastrophic as to cause marked distress in almost anyone'.[17] The person suffering from PTSD repeatedly relives the trauma with intrusive memories, flashbacks or nightmares, and they develop a sense of emotional numbness and detachment from other people. They avoid situations reminiscent of the trauma, and they are left in a state of hyperarousal – ever vigilant – so that they react to any unexpected noise or movement and suffer insomnia.

Box 5.4 Core features of post-traumatic stress disorder[17]

- Exposure to a traumatic event
- Avoidance of any reminiscent situation
- Reliving of the event through flashbacks or nightmares
- Numbness or a sense of detachment from other people and one's surroundings
- Hyperarousal: enhanced startle reaction and insomnia

PTSD only occurs in a certain proportion of individuals who are exposed to a particular trauma. Some people appear to be predisposed to developing PTSD.

Treatment of post-traumatic stress disorder

We pointed out the dangers of inappropriately medicalising human distress in the preface to this book. That having been stated, there is evidence that cognitive behavioural therapies, exposure therapy and antidepressant drugs are all effective in treating PTSD. There is no evidence to suggest that in-patient programmes, drama therapy, affect management, psychodynamic psychotherapy, supportive counselling, hypnotherapy, antipsychotic drugs or carbamazepine are effective in treating PTSD.

Psychological treatments

Cognitive behavioural therapy (CBT)[20]

The basic techniques employed in CBT, which were described in Chapter 3, can also be used to treat PTSD. Cognitive behavioural treatments have also been shown to have a positive effect compared with no treatment. Cognitive behavioural therapy and exposure therapy have been found to reduce the symptoms of PTSD more than relaxation therapy, both immediately and at 3 months follow-up.

Eye movement desensitisation and reprocessing (EMDR)[20]

Eye movement desensitisation and reprocessing has been described in Chapter 3. Although there have been no systematic reviews and there is no evidence of a theoretical basis for this intervention, there is some limited evidence of its efficacy from several controlled trials. Different research studies have found that it was better than no treatment, it reduced the symptoms of PTSD more than relaxation therapy, and it reduced symptoms more than active listening therapy. Another research study found evidence that EMDR was less effective than CBT.

Affect management

This involves managing mood. There is limited evidence that psychotherapy combined with drug treatment and affect management led to greater symptom control than psychotherapy plus drug treatment alone. There is no evidence of a significant difference in the effectiveness of psychodynamic psychotherapy, exposure therapy, and hypnotherapy for PTSD.

Other treatments that have been recommended include assertiveness training, debriefing as soon as possible, counselling and stress inoculation.[21]

Pharmacological treatment[20]

Although psychological interventions have been the mainstay of treatment for PTSD, there is growing evidence of the benefits of pharmacotherapy. One systematic review of drug treatments for PTSD found that fluoxetine, phenelzine, tricyclic antidepressants and the anxiolytic alprazolam were more effective in reducing symptoms than placebo. Alprazolam was the least effective drug. There is insufficient evidence for the effectiveness of antipsychotic drugs or carbamazepine.

Box 5.5 summarises the drug treatment of PTSD.

Box 5.5 Drug treatment of post-traumatic stress disorder (modified from Wilkinson *et al.*[17])

Core symptoms
- SSRI – for example, paroxetine 20–40 mg daily for 6 months or fluoxetine 20–40 mg daily for 6 months

Ineffective/poorly tolerated first-tried antidepressant
- Change to a different class of antidepressant at a therapeutic dose
- Consider specialist referral

Augmentation of drug therapy
- Lithium – poor impulse control
- Carbamazepine – persistent positive symptoms or aggression
- Propranolol – physiological hyperarousal (marked 'jumpiness')
- Clonidine – hyperarousal
- Benzodiazepines – severe anxiety/insomnia (use with caution)

Reflection exercises

Exercise 10 (for practice managers in liaison with clinicians in the practice team)

Look out all of the patient literature that you have in your practice for people with stress and other mental health problems. Does the literature match the most up-to-date thinking about best practice in stress management? Or does it promote out-of-date practices and approaches, or use old terminology? You will need to be clear yourself what the most up-to-date recommendations are in order to be able to check your literature and complete this exercise.

Exercise 11 (for practice managers, receptionists and others in the practice team)

Find out what initiatives have been undertaken by any of the practice team in order to ascertain patients' views during the previous 12 months. This might have included surveying or involving anyone registered with the practice (e.g. regular patients, people who do not use the services, carers) or the local community. How was the information obtained from the initiative used? Did changes result? Your own or practice team members' learning needs from this exercise might include the following:

(i) learning more about the variety of methods that can be employed to find out patients' views

(ii) learning how to apply any of those methods to find out the views of people with stress or other mental health problems about the care or services that are provided or that they wish to receive

(iii) learning more about organising a survey so that the findings are useful when making changes to the way in which services are planned or delivered, or staff behave

(iv) learning more about involving individual patients in decision making about the management of their mental health problems.

Now that you have completed these interactive reflection exercises, transfer the information about your learning needs to the relevant section in the empty template on pages 151–161 if you are working on your own personal development plan, or to the practice personal and professional development plan on pages 174–181 if you are working on a practice team learning plan. Don't forget to keep the evidence of your learning in your personal portfolio.

References

1 Richards C (1989) *The Health of Doctors.* King's Fund, London.
2 Chambers R (1999) *Survival Skills for GPs.* Radcliffe Medical Press, Oxford.
3 Cox T (1993) *Stress Research and Stress Management: Putting Theory to Work.* Health and Safety Executive Contract Research Report No. 61/1993. University of Nottingham, Nottingham.
4 Borrill C and Haynes C (2000) Stressed to kill. *Health Service J.* **10 February**: 24–5.
5 Sibbald B and Young R (2000) Job stress and mental health of GPs. *Br J Gen Pract.* **50**: 1007–8.
6 Clarke D (1989) *Stress Management.* National Extension College, Cambridge.
7 Chambers R and Davies M (1999) *What Stress in Primary Care!* Royal College of General Practitioners, London.
8 Haslam D (ed.) (2000) *Not Another Guide to Stress in General Practice.* Radcliffe Medical Press, Oxford.
9 Firth-Cozens J and Payne R (eds) (1999) *Stress in Health Professionals.* John Wiley & Sons Ltd, Chichester.
10 Reed F (1993) Mental health problems at work. *BMJ.* **306**: 1082.
11 Rosengren A, Orth-Gomer K, Wedel H *et al.* (1993) Stressful life events, social support, and mortality in men born in 1933. *BMJ.* **307**: 1102–5.
12 Stahl SM and Hauger RL (1994) Stress: an overview of the literature with emphasis on job-related strain and intervention. *Adv Ther.* **11**: 110–19.
13 Sims J (1997) The evaluation of stress management strategies in general practice: an evidence-led approach. *Br J Gen Pract.* **47**: 577–82.
14 Ernst E and Kanji N (2000) Autogenic training for stress and anxiety: a systematic review. *Compl Ther Med J.* **8**: 106–10.
15 Saunders T, Driskell JE, Johnston JH *et al.* (1996) The effect of stress inoculation training on anxiety and performance. *J Occup Health Psychol.* **1(2)**: 170–86.

16 Chambers R, George V, McNeill A *et al.* (1998) Health at work in the general practice. *Br J Gen Pract.* **48**: 1501–4.

17 Wilkinson G, Moore B and Moore P (2000) *Treating People with Anxiety and Stress.* Radcliffe Medical Press, Oxford.

18 Meichenbaum D (1985) *Stress Inoculation Training.* Pergamon Press, New York.

19 Meichenbaum D (1993) Stress inoculation training: a 20-year update. In RL Woolfolk and PM Lehrer (eds) *Principles and Practices of Stress Management.* Guilford Press, New York.

20 Barton S (ed.) (2001) *Clinical evidence. Issue 5.* BMJ Publishing Group, London.

21 Hale A (1997) Anxiety. ABC of mental health. *BMJ.* **314**: 1886–9.

CHAPTER 6

Schizophrenia

How common is schizophrenia?

Schizophrenia is one of the commonest forms of severe mental illness. Approximately one in every 100 people worldwide is affected by schizophrenia before they reach the age of 45 years. It is a major challenge for those working in primary care because of the frequency, the long duration of the illness, the severity of the disability it can cause from the perspectives of both the patient with schizophrenia and their family, and the high economic costs of providing health and social care.[1,2]

An estimated 250 000 people living in the UK are suffering from schizophrenia at any one time. The incidence varies with age, being about one in 10 000 per year, the highest rates being in young men aged 16 to 25 years and in women aged 26 to 36 years. Men usually develop a more severe form of the illness. The prevalence worldwide is thought to be 2–4 per 1000.[1–4] The rates are higher in people who live in inner-city areas.

African-Caribbean people living in the UK are diagnosed as having schizophrenia 3 to 12 times more often than the white population.[1] There is controversy about the extent to which genetic susceptibility accounts for the higher incidence, or whether it is due to economic deprivation or psychosocial factors, or even whether diagnosis does not take African-Caribbean cultural differences into account.[1] No specific gene for schizophrenia has been identified.

Box 6.1 Incidence and prevalence of schizophrenia in the UK

For every 100 000 people in the general population of the UK:

- up to 20 new cases of schizophrenia can be expected per year (the *incidence*)
- up to 400 people will suffer from schizophrenia in the course of a year (the *prevalence*).[2]

What is schizophrenia?

There is no specific physical test for schizophrenia. Diagnosis is made on the basis of the presence of symptoms and signs.

Schizophrenia affects a person's thinking, behaviour and feelings. There are two main groups of symptoms:

- *positive symptoms*, which include auditory and visual hallucinations (and might also include hallucinations of taste, smell or feel), delusions, disordered thinking (one thought does not follow logically from its predecessor, or connect to those that follow) and catatonic movements (the patient may be motionless, adopt odd postures, or be very excited or agitated)
- *negative symptoms* which include demotivation, self-neglect (e.g. inability to care about oneself, get out of bed, wash and dress), a tendency to withdraw from social contact, difficulty in communicating with others, and reduced emotion.[4]

The criteria for diagnosing schizophrenia are listed in Box 6.2 below. The International Classification of Diseases (ICD-10) that is given there emphasises symptoms such as hallucinatory voices commenting on the person's actions, delusions, experiences of interference with the person's thoughts, incoherent or irrelevant speech, changes in a person's ability to experience emotions, and a decline in their general level of functioning.

Box 6.2 ICD-10 criteria for diagnosing schizophrenia[3]

At least one of the following must be present:

- thought echo, insertion or withdrawal, or thought broadcasting
- delusions of control, influence or passivity, delusional perceptions (e.g. that secret agents are watching or listening)
- hallucinations, especially hallucinatory voices (e.g. giving a running commentary on the patient's behaviour, or discussing the patient)
- persistent delusions of other kinds that are completely impossible (e.g. controlling the weather).

Alternatively, at least two of the following must be present for most of the time during an episode of psychotic illness lasting

---

for at least one month, or at some time during most of the days:

- persistent hallucinations in any modality
- neologism (coining new words) or interpolations in the train of thought, resulting in incoherent or irrelevant speech
- catatonic behaviour, negativism, mutism and stupor
- 'negative' symptoms such as marked apathy, blunting or incongruity of emotional responses, other than symptoms due to depression or medication.'

Many of those who go on to develop schizophrenia experience prodromal symptoms between 6 and 12 months or occasionally 2 years before their first psychotic episode. These prodromal symptoms are non-specific and include impaired concentration, anxiety, a vague sense of unease, depression, anxiety, moodiness, social withdrawal, loss of interest or motivation, impaired function at school or work, self-injury or suicide attempts, suspiciousness, rebelliousness, alcohol or drug abuse and uncharacteristic aggression. Not everyone with these symptoms goes on to develop schizophrenia, as many of the symptoms are non-specific and common in adolescence.

What causes schizophrenia?

Risk factors are thought to include a family history – people with a sibling or parent with schizophrenia are 10 times as likely to have the illness, too. However, most people with schizophrenia do not have an affected relative. Other causes of schizophrenia for which there is some evidence that is not yet conclusive include: brain damage at or around birth, exposure to certain viruses during pregnancy, development difficulties, central nervous system infections in childhood, cannabis use and acute life events – which may precipitate the illness or a relapse.[1,4]

Schizophrenia is thought to be mediated through excess amounts of one of the brain's main neurotransmitters, namely dopamine, being secreted.

Course of the illness

About 25% of people who develop schizophrenia recover well within five years with no need for further drug treatment. The illness and associated problems of about a further half to two-thirds fluctuate over decades, with better periods when the patient is functioning reasonably well. The other 10–15% of cases develop severe persistent incapacity and are significantly disabled by the illness.[1,2]

The outcome seems to be worse for people in whom the disease has an insidious onset, where treatment is delayed, with social isolation, or with a strong family history.[4] People who misuse drugs may also have a worse outcome.

Co-existing depression is common.

About 10% of patients with schizophrenia commit suicide, and two to three times this number make suicide attempts. The risk of suicide is 8.5 times higher than that of the general population. Twice as many men with schizophrenia commit suicide as women. Suicide is most common:

- within the first 10 years of diagnosis
- with continued relapses in the course of the illness
- during in-patient stays or soon after discharge
- when there have been previous suicidal attempts
- if there is coexisting depression or substance abuse
- if the patient lacks social support.

Patients who have good insight into their condition are also more prone to committing suicide.[1,3]

Other reasons for the high mortality rate in patients with schizophrenia, in addition to suicide, are accidents, and diseases of the heart, respiratory and digestive systems. People with schizophrenia are more likely than the general population to abuse alcohol or drugs, or to smoke.[3]

Box 6.3 The homeless mentally ill[1]

In one study conducted in 1995 in London, half of those who were homeless had schizophrenia. Most of them had received treatment at some time, but one-sixth had never consulted a mental health professional.

Other studies undertaken in hostels for the homeless have found that one-third to two-thirds of new arrivals have schizophrenia.

The costs

Costs might be reduced if there was earlier recognition of schizophrenia and thus earlier active intervention. One report on the costs of care of patients with schizophrenia in England gave an estimate of £810 million in 1992–93.[3] The use of atypical antipsychotic drugs as a first-line treatment could add about £210 million to the annual UK drug budget if these drugs were prescribed for everyone with schizophrenia, and £54 million if they were given to all of those with treatment-resistant schizophrenia (as estimated in 1998).[5] Overall, the economic evidence is inconclusive as to whether there are net savings in the overall costs of treating people with schizophrenia with the newer, more expensive antipsychotic drugs.

A study of 193 patients with schizophrenia or paranoid illnesses in Scotland found that the direct costs for their care exceeded £1.2 million over a 6-month period in the mid-1990s.[2]

Indirect costs of schizophrenia are thought to exceed the direct costs of providing health and social care by several-fold. Indirect costs include lost employment, and the costs of families caring for the person with schizophrenia. The National Schizophrenia Fellowship (NSF) estimates that informal carers such as parents and other relatives save UK governments around £3 billion a year.

Caring in the community

The Care Programme Approach (CPA) in England, or care plan guidelines elsewhere, sets out to assess and meet the health and social care needs of each individual (*see* Box 6.4).

Box 6.4 The Care Programme Approach (CPA)[6]

This scheme includes the following:

- systematic arrangements for the assessment of the health and social needs of the patient
- appointment of a key worker
- a written care plan that addresses identified needs and is agreed with the patient
- regular review and changes to the plan, as required.

The key worker is a trained mental health professional (not a GP) who is responsible for acting as a focal contact for the patient, carer and others, arranging the needs assessment, drawing up the care plan, and co-ordinating mental, physical and social care.

The CPA has three levels:

1 a minimal care programme for people with limited healthcare needs arising from their mental illness – they are likely to be stable and require intervention from only one member of the specialist services
2 a more complex, intermediate care programme for patients who require moderate levels of support. Several members of the specialist mental health service may be involved in providing care
3 a full multidisciplinary care programme for patients who suffer from severe mental illness, whose needs are volatile and who represent a significant risk to themselves and others. A consultant psychiatrist will decide whether the patient should be placed on the local supervision register for 'at-risk' people.

Patients with schizophrenia need good healthcare, day care, employment and housing. Day centres help patients with the skills of daily living (e.g. hygiene, housework and budget planning), job training and help in finding employment.

The key worker from the community psychiatric team has a special responsibility for the patient, co-ordinating with other agencies as necessary. Members of a community psychiatric team should include a community psychiatric nurse, psychologist, psychiatrist, social worker, occupational therapist and non-clinical support staff. Support from not-for-profit agencies or voluntary services is very valuable (*see* Appendix for contact details of many support and help groups).

With assertive community treatment, patients are diverted to the care of a community-based multidisciplinary team. The team sees patients in their own homes and provides 24-hour cover and 'assertive outreach'. This means that they continue to contact their patients and offer services even when the patients are reluctant or unco-operative. Assertive outreach reduces the likelihood of admission to hospital.

Box 6.5 Assertive community treatment – how it works in practice[8]

In one London-based mental health trust, a multidisciplinary team provides assertive outreach, risk management, treatment and care for people with severe mental illness outside hospital to ensure that contact is maintained and effective treatment is delivered. The team prioritises those interventions for which there is evidence of effectiveness, namely clozapine medication, schizophrenia family work, support for carers, maintaining stable accommodation, minimising social stressors and administering supervised medication.

The Assertive Community Treatment (ACT) team targets those most in need and maintains frequent contacts with clients in their own homes and neighbourhoods. Supervised medication and early intervention can be provided when crises occur. The key worker can provide practical assistance (e.g. transporting clients to activities and promoting daily living skills).

Treatment of schizophrenia

A patient with newly diagnosed schizophrenia should be referred urgently to a psychiatrist. In some cases, the patient may be reluctant to accept help, especially if they are in the midst of an acute phase with florid delusions and hallucinations and are hostile to health professionals. The treating GP may need to invoke the reformed Mental Health Act, although they should involve the community mental health team's expertise and avoid compulsory care if possible.

Drug treatment is more likely to be successful in combating positive symptoms than negative ones. Up to one-third of patients with schizophrenia derive little benefit from drug treatment. About 50% of patients with schizophrenia do not adhere to prescribed drug treatment in the short term, and even more fail to take their medication in the longer term. Depot preparations have been manufactured to aid compliance, but little difference has been found in the results in trials of oral vs. depot administration of antipsychotic drugs.[5]

Polypharmacy is common. Patients with schizophrenia often experience depression, for which they are prescribed antidepressant drugs, and they often experience side-effects from their antipsychotic drugs, for which they are prescribed anticholinergic medication. This may lead to intolerable drug interactions and side-effects. Typical antipsychotic drugs have side-effects such as severe extrapyramidal effects that cause muscle spasms, muscle shaking and tremor and feelings of inner restlessness. Atypical antipsychotic drugs have side-effects such as sexual dysfunction, excessive weight gain, loss of energy and sedation. The *Maudsley Prescribing Guidelines* strongly recommend prescription of one antipsychotic drug at a time.[8]

Box 6.6 People's views on medication and other interventions for mental illness[8]

A total of 2222 people responded to a survey organised by the National Schizophrenia Fellowship (NSF), MIND and the Manic Depression Fellowship (MDF), of whom 37% reported that they had schizophrenia. Nearly half (44%) of those on medication had stopped taking it without the support of their doctor.

People who received the older type of medication were given less information, and were also given less choice by professionals about alternative medication, than those on the newer atypical antipsychotics.

Over 16% of patients with schizophrenia were on two or more antipsychotic drugs.

Antipsychotic drugs, also known as neuroleptics, are the mainstay of treatment for schizophrenia. Several different drugs are effective in the treatment of schizophrenia, and the advantages and drawbacks of these are outlined in Table 6.1[4,5].

Although they offer the advantages of fewer adverse effects, the newer antipsychotics are more expensive. As yet there is no evidence that this increased cost is offset by a reduction in indirect costs such as hospitalisation.[5]

Typical antipsychotic drugs[4,9,10]

These drugs work mainly by blocking the activity of the D_2 receptors for the neurotransmitter dopamine. The best known are chlorpromazine (a phenothiazine) and haloperidol (a butyrophenone). They are available in a range of doses and formulations, including oral medication and depot injections. The injections may be given by the community psychiatric nurse in the patient's home or at a community clinic.

Table 6.1 Characteristics of typical versus atypical antipsychotic drugs[4,9,10]

Classification of antipsychotic drug	Recommended dose range	Adverse effects and extent compared with the other type of drug
Typical antipsychotic drugs		
Chlorpromazine	75–300 mg daily	More sedation, acute dystonias, parkinsonism, weight gain, skin photosensitivity, dizziness, jaundice, dry mouth, blood dyscrasias
Haloperidol decanoate	50–100 mg every 4 weeks	More dry mouth, blurred vision, constipation, dizziness, impotence, sedation, acute dystonias, parkinsonism, weight gain, skin photosensitivity, jaundice, blood dyscrasias
Pipothiazine palmitate	50–100 mg every 4 weeks	As for chlorpromazine
Atypical antipsychotic drugs		
Olanzapine	5–20 mg daily	More increase in appetite and weight gain Less extrapyramidal adverse effects, vomiting, insomnia and drowsiness
Risperidone	4–6 mg daily	More weight gain Less extrapyramidal adverse effects and daytime somnolence
Clozapine	150–300 mg daily	More hypersalivation, temperature increases and sedation Less dry mouth, blood dyscrasias and extrapyramidal adverse effects
Quetiapine	300–450 mg daily	More dry mouth and sleepiness Less dystonia
Zotepine	75–300 mg daily	More clinically important improvement Less akathisia

Chlorpromazine

Chlorpromazine is an effective antipsychotic drug in the immediate, short and medium term. However, adverse effects such as sedation, acute dystonias and parkinsonism, weight gain, skin photosensitivity, dizziness, jaundice, dry mouth and blood dyscrasias can affect the patient's functioning and for this reason may make it unacceptable to many people.

Depot haloperidol decanoate

Intramuscular depot haloperidol decanoate was found to be more effective than placebo in one study.[4]

Depot pipothiazine palmitate

Intramuscular depot pipothiazine palmitate seems to be as effective as standard antipsychotic drugs in the treatment of schizophrenia.

Extrapyramidal side-effects

- Acute dystonia – usually facial grimacing and torticollis, and sometimes an oculogyric crisis from spasm of the ocular muscles. It is treated by procyclidine or other anticholinergic drugs. Acute dystonia tends to occur soon after treatment with antipsychotic drugs has been started.
- Akathisia – restlessness. It is treated by reducing the dose of antipsychotic drug. This tends to occur several weeks after treatment has started.
- Parkinsonism – tremor, bradykinesia and rigidity. It is either treated with antiparkinsonism drugs or it may resolve spontaneously. It tends to occur several weeks or months after starting treatment with antipsychotic drugs.
- Tardive dyskinesia – facial movements such as grimacing and chewing, and choreo–athetoid movements. It tends to occur several years after starting antipsychotic drugs, and it may not resolve even if the trigger drugs are reduced or discontinued.

Newer (atypical) antipsychotic drugs[4]

These drugs may cause fewer extrapyramidal side-effects and be more acceptable to patients with schizophrenia than standard (typical) antipsychotic drugs such as chlorpromazine and haloperidol. Atypical antipsychotic drugs target receptors for the neurotransmitters serotonin and noradrenaline.

  No atypical antipsychotic drug is marketed as a depot injection, but risperidone is available as a liquid and olanzapine is available as a dispersible preparation that dissolves in the mouth.

Risperidone

Risperidone has been found to be more effective than standard antipsychotic drugs (usually haloperidol) in treating schizophrenia, and it has fewer adverse effects. There is no evidence that risperidone is more effective than other new antipsychotic drugs.

Quetiapine

Quetiapine is as effective as standard antipsychotic drugs, and although it has similar adverse effects, it causes less dystonia than standard antipsychotics. However, more patients report a dry mouth and sleepiness.

Clozapine

Clozapine is used for patients with schizophrenia who are resistant to other antipsychotic medication.

It is more effective than standard antipsychotic drugs in both the short and long term. However, clozapine is more likely than standard antipsychotic drugs to cause hypersalivation, temperature increases and sedation, although it is less likely to cause dry mouth or extrapyramidal adverse effects than are standard antipsychotic drugs.

There is no evidence of a difference in effectiveness or safety between clozapine and the other new antipsychotic drugs, namely olanzapine and risperidone. Clozapine is associated with potentially fatal blood problems, but despite the need for regular blood tests, it seems to be more acceptable than standard antipsychotic drugs.

Patients who are taking clozapine should have a white-blood-cell count checked every week during the first 18 weeks of treatment, every 2 weeks for one year, and every month thereafter.[3]

Olanzapine

Olanzapine is more effective than standard antipsychotic drugs such as haloperidol. It causes fewer extrapyramidal adverse effects, less nausea and vomiting and less insomnia and drowsiness than standard antipsychotic drugs. However, it is associated with a greater increase in appetite and weight gain than are standard antipsychotic drugs.

Olanzapine does not seem to be any more effective than any of the other new antipsychotic drugs, but it has fewer adverse effects. For instance, it has fewer extrapyramidal adverse effects, and causes less parkinsonism and less need for anticholinergic medication than risperidone, although olanzapine does lead to a greater weight gain, and there are more reports of dry mouth than with risperidone.

Psychosocial interventions

Although medication is the mainstay of treatment for schizophrenia, around 5–25% of patients who take medication continue to experience symptoms of schizophrenia,[11-13] and many of them experience adverse side-effects.[10] For this reason, a variety of psychological, nursing and occupational therapies have been shown to be effective adjuncts in treating schizophrenia.[14] These include the following:

- family intervention
- life skills programmes
- cognitive behavioural therapy
- cognitive rehabilitation
- psychodynamic psychotherapy and psychoanalysis
- social skills programmes.

Box 6.7

The percentage of patients with schizophrenia who had tried a non-medical intervention in one survey of 2200 people[8] with a mental illness ranged from 19% (homeopathy or herbal medicine) to 56% (talking therapy). The percentages of those who found the therapy 'helpful or very helpful' were as follows:

- exercise and training/education – 85%
- art or music – 81%
- talking treatments – 79%
- cognitive behavioural therapy – 72%
- nutrition or diet – 70%
- homeopathy or herbal medicine – 61%.

Family intervention for schizophrenia

Research has shown that people with schizophrenia who come from families that express high levels of criticism, hostility or over-involvement have more frequent relapses than individuals with similar symptoms who come from families that are less expressive of their emotions. Family intervention is an adjunct to drug treatment that aims to decrease the relapse rate in patients by 'treating' the family. This involves psychotherapy aimed at improving the atmosphere within the family by reducing levels of stress, anger and guilt.

There is limited research evidence that family intervention may encourage adherence to medication, help reduce relapse rates, and decrease rates of hospitalisation or the tendency of individuals or families to drop out of care. Family intervention may improve social impairment and the levels of expressed emotion within the family.

However, there is no evidence that it affects the suicide rate of patients with schizophrenia.[15]

Life skills programmes for chronic mental illnesses

Life skills programmes are often a part of the rehabilitation process and they address the needs associated with independent functioning, such as training in managing money, organising and running a home, domestic skills and personal self-care. The evidence for the benefits of life skills programmes is inconclusive.[16]

Cognitive behavioural therapy (CBT)

CBT combined with standard care is more effective than standard care alone in reducing relapse rates.[17,18] However, there is no evidence that CBT improves compliance with medication, or that it is any more or less effective than supportive psychotherapy.

Cognitive rehabilitation, psychodynamic psychotherapy, psychoanalysis and social skills training

There is no broad consensus on the efficacy of non-medical interventions, as too little well-planned research has been undertaken. There is no evidence that cognitive rehabilitation is more effective than a placebo intervention in influencing mental state, social behaviour or cognitive functioning.[19]

There have been no research trials assessing the effectiveness of psychoanalytical approaches for the treatment of schizophrenia, and there is only very limited data on the effectiveness of psychodynamic approaches. There is no evidence of any positive effect of psychodynamic therapy, and the possibility of adverse effects seems never to have been considered. The psychodynamic approach may be more acceptable to patients than a more cognitive reality-adaptive therapy.[20]

Social skills training is a treatment strategy aimed at developing more effective social communication, enhancing social performance and reducing the distress and difficulty experienced in social situations by people with a diagnosis of schizophrenia. Verbal and non-verbal communication, and the individual's ability to perceive and respond to social cues, are assessed and addressed via modelling, role-play and social reinforcement.

Reducing relapse rates in schizophrenia[4]

Not only are relapses distressing for the sufferer and their family, but the frequency with which a person relapses may have an overall negative effect on their long-term mental health. Once a patient has reached an optimum level of functioning, it is essential that they are assisted in maintaining that level. Health professionals working in primary care play a significant role in preventing serious relapse. There is evidence that the following four interventions can reduce relapse rates in schizophrenia:

- continued treatment with antipsychotic drugs
- family interventions
- social skills training
- cognitive behavioural therapy.

Relapse rates are significantly reduced by continuing antipsychotic medication for at least 6 months after an acute episode. The benefits of this are apparent for up to 2 years.[20] Patients who have had more than one episode of psychosis should receive maintenance therapy for at least 3 years after the last episode of psychosis.[3]

Although there is no evidence of a difference in relapse rates between standard antipsychotic drugs, one report found that relapse rates over 6–24 months were significantly lower in patients taking chlorpromazine than in those on placebo.[4] Family intervention involving education about schizophrenia and training in problem solving over at least six weekly sessions has been found to reduce relapse rates significantly.[4]

Social skills training (e.g. instruction and rehearsal in social interaction) may reduce relapse rates. However, motivation is an important predictor of benefit from social skills training. Cognitive behavioural therapy combined with standard care may reduce relapse rates.

Providing services for patients with severe mental illness, including schizophrenia

The National Service Framework for Mental Health sets standards for effective services for patients with severe mental illness in England. These standards have been drawn up to try to prevent and anticipate crises whenever possible, and they are generalisable to the rest of the UK. They should ensure prompt and effective help if a crisis does occur, with good access to an appropriate and safe mental health placement if necessary, as close to the patient's home as possible. Standards 4 and 5 relate to the service provided by mental health trusts. Those in primary care need to co-ordinate referral and discharge arrangements, and to share ongoing care and monitoring.[21]

The National Institute for Clinical Excellence (NICE) is currently reviewing local and national guidelines to recommend 'kitemark examples of good practice'.[22]

Primary care organisations have a duty to provide effective mental health services for patients with severe mental illness. An effective clinical governance network and the involvement of users and carers are central to developing the service. The more closely that a primary care organisation works with the local mental health trust, the voluntary sector and social services, the better co-ordinated will be the care provided for patients from pooled resources.[22]

Health services and community agencies need to collaborate to reduce the length of time for which patients with psychosis remain untreated.[23]

Reform of the Mental Health Act 1983

Mental health trusts should be reviewing their arrangements for monitoring of this Act to check that infringements of liberty carried out under current legislation in the Mental Health Act (MHA) are in line with the Human Rights Act that came into force in October 2000. Such monitoring should include the proportion of people from ethnic minorities who are detained, as well as the frequency of use of the MHA.

Using the MHA to detain a person in hospital is a fundamental infringement of an individual's civil liberties and its use must be lawful, as minimally restrictive as possible, and consistent with best practice.

Box 6.8

There should be monitoring of informal personal restraint in hospitals and nursing homes which are outside the remit of the MHA – through the locking of ward or bedroom doors, medication, seclusion and targeted physical restraint that traps the individual in their chair or bed, etc. (a practice that is euphemistically known by some as 'therapeutic handling').

New mental health legislation in England will provide a single framework for the application of compulsory powers for care and treatment. It covers the quality and consistency of health and social care services for patients who suffer from mental health problems.[24] This will include the following:

- common criteria
- a common pathway for assessment
- the approval of a plan of care and treatment by the Mental Health Tribunal after 28 days of compulsory detention (to protect patients' rights)
- an improved and more consistent set of safeguards for all patients.

Part One of the White Paper[24] is the new legal framework that describes how the new mental health legislation will operate for compulsory care in the community. Part Two sets out separate arrangements for 'high-risk' patients or the small minority of patients who pose a significant risk of serious harm to other people as a result of their mental disorders.

There will be a new structure for the application of compulsory powers of detention for assessment and treatment of 'high-risk' patients. Compulsory treatment powers will be extended from hospitals into the community, so that patients who refuse to comply with community treatment programmes can be compulsorily sent back to hospital.

GPs may have to work more closely in organising compulsory treatment and assessing and drawing up care plans for patients who require compulsory treatment in the community, as a result of the new legislation. Preliminary assessments and compulsory care plans will be drawn up by a team of two doctors, one of whom may be the patient's GP, and a social worker or another approved mental health professional.

Box 6.9

Throughout the consultation about the reform of the Mental Health Act the important role of carers has been emphasised, and the need to involve them in planning care and treatment, and to offer them all necessary support. Standard 6 of the NSF promotes improvements in the way in which carers are regarded and their well-being is monitored and addressed.

Reflection exercises

Exercise 12 (for the practice team)

Undertake an analysis of the strengths, weaknesses, opportunities and threats (SWOT) of the way in which your practice operates its systems and procedures for managing patients with severe mental illness. This will involve convening a group to represent all elements of your practice team (e.g. GP, nurse, manager/support staff, community psychiatric nurse and community pharmacist). You will be considering the following:

(i) your infrastructure – capacity for computerised recall, the practice protocol, access and availability of any special mental health-promoting clinics, hardware and software, information resources, and the existence of disease registers, (e.g. a practice register of those patients known to have schizophrenia or other psychoses).

(ii) your capability – staff numbers and posts, and skills (clinical skills, personal and communication skills and IT skills)

(iii) your capacity – how you cope with demand and availability of the community mental health team

(iv) the extent to which you work as a team across the practice, with others from the mental health trust or the voluntary or independent sectors, and most of all with patients – including responding to feedback in order to achieve patient-centred care.

Use the 14 components of clinical governance described in Chapter 1 as a check-list for the SWOT analysis.

Then make a plan for improvement. This should include what you need to learn (transfer your needs and action plan to your personal and practice development plans), what you need to buy, who you need to appoint or involve and what you need to reorganise.

Exercise 13 (for GPs)

Invite the local psychiatrist specialising in the treatment and management of psychoses to visit the practice for an in-house educational session. Discuss the last five referral letters written to the psychiatrist or community psychiatric nurse about patients with schizophrenia and the five most recent letters from the consultant or nurse to the practice. Could you have done more in the practice? Were the responding letters from the trust staff appropriate? Were they informative enough? Do they need to learn more about the problems of general practice? Ask the consultant to review your practice protocol and discuss how to provide more seamless care for patients, shifting work and resources to primary care as far as possible.

Invite the local community pharmacists, community psychiatric nurse, psychologist, counsellors and workers from local mental health self-help groups to join you for this educational session, and positively encourage them to contribute to the discussions.

Exercise 14 (for GPs)

Conduct an audit of the process of management of patients with schizophrenia in your practice, in order to determine the proportion of patients who are known to have schizophrenia and who have had an annual review. With regard to the annual review, consider the following questions.

- Was the patient's continued use of antipsychotic drugs assessed?
- Was the patient encouraged to comply with treatment?
- Was the patient's general health assessed?
- Were side-effects from their prescribed medication enquired about?
- Were other drugs being taken (prescribed or illicit substances)?
- Was the patient a smoker of cigarettes and, if so, was advice about smoking cessation given?
- Was the patient receiving care and regular contact from a community mental health team, or an assertive outreach team?
- Was the well-being of any carer's health enquired about and family therapy offered if appropriate?
- Were appropriate blood tests performed regularly for patients taking clozapine?
- Was a patient who might be contemplating a planned pregnancy or who might be at risk of an unplanned pregnancy advised about the potentially harmful effects of their medication, or was referral to a genetics expert arranged if appropriate?

Now that you have completed these interactive reflection exercises, transfer the information about your learning needs to the relevant section in the empty template on pages 151–161 if you are working on your own personal development plan, or to the practice personal and professional development plan on pages 174–181 if you are working on a practice team learning plan. Don't forget to keep the evidence of your learning in your personal portfolio.

References

1 National Schizophrenia Fellowship (1996) *Schizophrenia and Research – UK*. Factsheet 6. National Schizophrenia Fellowship, Kingston upon Thames.
2 Stark C (2000) Schizophrenia: public health aspects. In: *Schizophrenia. The role of atypical antipsychotics in management and delivering the NSF objectives: focus on olanzapine.* A and M Publishing Ltd, Guildford.
3 Baker R, Brugha T and Khunti K (1999) *Primary Care of People With Schizophrenia. Audit protocol CT14.* Clinical Governance Research and Development Unit, University of Leicester, Leicester.
4 Barton S (2001) *Clinical Evidence. Issue 5.* BMJ Publishing Group, London.
5 Adams C (ed.) (1999) Drug treatments for schizophrenia. In: *Effective Health Care Bulletin.* NHS Centre for Reviews and Dissemination, University of York, York.
6 Cohen A and Paton J (1999) *A Workbook for Primary Care Groups. Developing an integrated mental health service.* Sainsbury Centre for Mental Health, London.
7 NHS Beacon Services (2000) *NHS Beacon Learning Handbook 2000/2001. Volume 1.* NHS Beacon Services, Petersfield.
8 National Schizophrenia Fellowship (2000) *A Question of Choice.* National Schizophrenia Fellowship, Kingston upon Thames.
9 Mehta D (ed.) (2001) *British National Formulary.* British Medical Association and Royal Pharmaceutical Society of Great Britain, London.
10 Duggan L, Fenton M, Dardennes RM *et al.* (2000) Olanzapine for schizophrenia. In: *The Cochrane Library. Issue 2.* Update Software, Oxford.
11 Christison GW, Kirch DG and Wyatt RJ (1991) When symptoms persist: choosing among alternative somatic symptoms for schizophrenia. *Schizophr Bull.* **17**: 217–45.
12 Meltzer HY (1992) Treatment of the neuroleptic-non-responsive schizophrenic patient. *Schizophr Bull.* **18**: 515–42.
13 Davis JM and Casper R (1997) Antipsychotic drugs: clinical pharmacology and therapeutic use. *Drugs.* **14**: 260–82.
14 Thompson P (ed.) (2000) *Schizophrenia: a workbook for healthcare professionals.* Radcliffe Medical Press, Oxford.
15 Pharaoh FM, Mari JJ and Streiner D (2000) Family intervention for schizophrenia. In: *The Cochrane Library. Issue 2.* Update Software, Oxford.
16 Nicol MM, Robertson L and Connaughton JA (2000) Life skills programmes for chronic mental illnesses (Cochrane Review). In: *The Cochrane Library. Issue 3.* Update Software, Oxford.
17 Beck AT (1970) *Depression: causes and treatment.* University of Pennsylvania Press, Philadelphia, PA.
18 Jones C, Cormac I, Mota J *et al.* (2000) Cognitive behavioural therapy for schizophrenia. In: *The Cochrane Library. Issue 2.* Update Software, Oxford.

19 Hayes RL and McGrath JJ (2000) Cognitive rehabilitation for people with schizophrenia and related conditions (Cochrane Review). In: *The Cochrane Library. Issue 3.* Update Software, Oxford.

20 Malmberg L and Fenton M (2000) Individual psychodynamic psychotherapy and psychoanalysis for schizophrenia and severe mental illness (Cochrane Review). In: *The Cochrane Library. Issue 3.* Update Software, Oxford.

21 NHS Executive (1999) *National Service Framework for Mental Health.* Department of Health, London.

22 Cohen A (2000) *Primary Care Mental Health.* HSJ Monograph No. 2. Emap Public Sector Management, London.

23 McGrath J and Emmerson WB (1999) Treatment of schizophrenia. *BMJ.* **319**: 1045–8.

24 Department of Health (2000) *Reforming the Mental Health Act.* Department of Health, London.

CHAPTER 7

Dementia

Kuljit Jheeta and Ruth Chambers

What is dementia?

Dementia is 'characterised by global impairment of cerebral function with preservation of clear consciousness'.[1] It is a chronic or progressive disturbance of multiple higher cortical functions, including memory, thinking, orientation, comprehension, calculation, learning capacity, language and judgement. Impairment of cognitive function is commonly accompanied (and occasionally preceded) by deterioration in emotional control, social behaviour or motivation.[2]

Symptoms of dementia usually develop slowly, but sometimes dementia does have a sudden onset as a result of a particular event or illness.

Dementia gradually affects an individual's ability to:

- remember things for more than a few seconds
- understand situations
- cope with everyday tasks
- express feelings
- think clearly in order to solve problems
- cope with an over-stimulating environment
- behave in the 'normal ways' that they have learned throughout their lives
- make decisions
- understand a sequence of complex tasks, eventually being unable to perform even simple tasks without help.

Box 7.1

Dementia results in loss of memory, loss of executive function and ability to make decisions, and changes in personality.[1]

How common is dementia?[2-5]

About 5% of people over 65 years of age and 20% of those over 80 years have some type of dementia. Around 600 000 people are estimated to suffer from dementia currently in the UK. On average, a GP practice with a patient population of 10 000 will have about 90 patients with dementia on its list.

The incidence of dementia is 1.6 new patients per general practitioner per year for a typical list of 2000 patients, with an average workload of 7.4 consultations per person with dementia per GP per year.

The number of people with dementia is expected to increase in the elderly population as a whole over the next two or three decades, as people are living longer.

The proportion of people with dementia roughly doubles for every five-year age band from 65 to 90 years of age. Recent estimates for England and Wales have been based on national census data and on surveys in six geographical areas. These surveys have found that the prevalence of dementia is 6% for the 75–79 years age group, but 13% for those aged 80–84 years, with increasing prevalence in those aged 85 years or over.

Dementia is more common in women than in men, especially in the older age groups, and the rate of cognitive problems is much higher in people of lower social classes. There is some evidence that individuals who have been educated to a higher level are less likely to experience Alzheimer's disease, and that its onset might be delayed.

Classification of dementia[3]

Dementia is classified according to the varying degrees of minimal, mild, moderate and severe dementia, which merge into each other.

Minimal dementia

A person with 'minimal' dementia has some difficulty in recalling recent events and may be prone to mislaying or losing things. They are usually still independent and care is probably not needed.

Mild dementia

A person with 'mild' dementia has most of the following signs and symptoms: difficulty in recalling recent information; limited or patchy disorientation in time and place; impaired problem solving, reasoning and ability to manage everyday activities. In the later stages of mild dementia some degree of care will usually be required.

Moderate dementia

A person with 'moderate' dementia has most of the following signs and symptoms: severely impaired reasoning, problem solving and recall of recent events; disorientation in time and place; speech slightly unclear, but not to a marked degree; inability to manage housework, shopping and finances independently; the need for help with dressing and other self-care; occasional incontinence. Daily care is usually required for those with moderate dementia.

Severe dementia

A person with 'severe' dementia is totally disorientated, incapable of recall, reasoning and self-care, unable to communicate in normal speech, may fail to recognise close relatives, and is almost invariably incontinent, apathetic and inert. The person with severe dementia may become immobile, and will be totally incapable of being independent. Continual care and supervision are usually required.

The need for care depends on how long an individual can continue to live alone or be independent. The needs of an individual tend to vary from one time to another, as there may be episodes of severely disturbed behaviour. Therefore health and social care services need to be flexible.

Types of dementia

There are over 70 types of dementia, but the two commonest types in older people are Alzheimer's disease and multi-infarct dementia (also known as vascular dementia). Both of these types of dementia are irreversible and cannot be cured, although there is some evidence to suggest that their deterioration may be slowed down with new drugs if they are diagnosed at an early stage.

The frequency of different causes of dementia in the UK is as follows:[1–6]

- Alzheimer's disease – 55–60%
- vascular dementia – 20%
- cortical Lewy body disease – 15%
- Pick's disease – 5%
- others – 5%.

Reversible types of dementia are found in only about 1% of patients. They most commonly include the following:

- neurological disorders – trauma, normal-pressure hydrocephalus and cerebral tumour
- systemic disorders – hypoxia, anaemia, liver failure and renal failure
- endocrine disorders – diabetes, thyroid disorders, Cushing's disease and parathyroid disorders
- vitamin deficiencies – vitamin B_{12} and thiamine.
- infective disorders (e.g. syphilis).

Alzheimer's disease[3]

Alzheimer's disease is the fourth commonest cause of death in the Western world, after heart disease, cancer and strokes. Over half of all dementia in the UK is of this type. The cost of treatment and care of people with Alzheimer's disease has been estimated to be about £6.1 billion per annum in the UK.

The main features are prominent and progressive memory impairment, conversational problems such as difficulties in finding the right words, disorientation in place (particularly in unfamiliar surroundings) and global cognitive impairment.

Alzheimer's disease is not a general term for dementia despite the fact that many of the general population use the term 'Alzheimer's' in an all-encompassing manner. It is a specific diagnosis. Alzheimer's disease is caused by damage to nerve cells in the brain – a defect in amyloid precursor protein leading to deposits of abnormal amyloid in the central nervous system.[1] The cognitive deterioration in Alzheimer's disease seems to be due to lower than normal levels of the neurotransmitter acetylcholine in the brain. This theory underpins the use of anticholinesterase drugs to increase the levels of available acetylcholine for symptomatic treatment.

There is some understanding of why these particular nerve cells are damaged. For some years it was thought that aluminum played a role, but this now seems less likely. It seems more probable that a chemical in the brain that normally helps to keep the brain healthy becomes

Patient's don't always understand the terminology we use.

toxic to the nerve cells, so that they do not function properly and may even die. Alzheimer's disease is not a normal part of ageing.

A small number of cases of Alzheimer's disease that occur in younger people are hereditary, and it is these genetic types of dementia that are helping researchers to determine what the toxic chemical is and how the damage is done.

People with Down's syndrome are more likely to develop Alzheimer's disease – up to 40% of those aged over 50 years have dementia.

Multi-infarct dementia (vascular dementia)

This is the second commonest type of dementia. Sufferers have damage to small areas of the brain, sometimes following a stroke or a series of small strokes. This damage may lead to vascular dementia. Alzheimer's disease and multi-infarct dementia can occur together.

Features that suggest vascular dementia include a recent history of a cerebrovascular accident, transient ischaemic attack or myocardial infarction, and the presence of vascular risk factors or focal neurological signs (these may indicate other causative conditions, too). Vascular dementia develops in a step-like way as minor vascular events occur, the type of damage depending on which area of the brain is affected. The risk factors for vascular dementia are hypertension, diabetes, smoking, previous cerebrovascular accident or transient ischaemic attack and atrial fibrillation.

Aspirin may help to prevent further vascular events in patients with a previous history of transient ischaemic attack or stroke.

Other types of dementia

In around 25% of people with dementia the disorder arises from conditions other than Alzheimer's disease or vascular dementia.

- Pick's disease affects the front of the brain, leading to loss of judgement and loss of inhibitions.
- Lewy body dementia is related to Parkinson's disease, and follows a different course to that of Alzheimer's disease, with fluctuating cognitive impairment, many spells of confusion, repeated falls, visual hallucinations and a rapid decline to death.

- Dementia occurs in the majority of cases of Huntington's chorea. This is an inherited degenerative brain disease that is gradually progressive.
- Some people with acquired immune deficiency syndrome (AIDS) develop dementia in the later stages of the illness. The AIDS virus itself may attack certain brain cells, and people with AIDS may develop viral infections of the brain because of their weakened immune system.
- The symptoms of Creutzfeldt-Jakob disease (CJD) are similar to those of Alzheimer's disease in about 10% of patients. An electroencephalogram (EEG) and analysis of the cerebrospinal fluid distinguishes the two conditions.

Course of the illness

One-third of all patients with dementia were in hospitals, residential care or nursing homes in 1996.[3] The number of patients with dementia in continuing-care establishments is predicted to increase by 14% over the next 10 years, assuming that the criteria for admission remain the same.

People with dementia live for about seven or eight years on average after the disorder has first been diagnosed, although there is wide individual variation. They and their families have to deal with the effects of dementia itself – not only the deterioration in memory, reasoning and ability, but also the changes in relationships and interactions as other people begin to treat them differently.

Many of the carers of older people with dementia are themselves fairly old. Around two-thirds of them are husbands or wives. Carers of patients with dementia generally experience greater stress than carers of people with other types of needs, nearly 50% having some kind of mental health problem themselves. The inability of carers to tolerate difficult behaviour is the critical factor in their seeking help from statutory services. Many feel that their needs for home support and medical care are not being fully met. The most difficult problems for carers to cope with are personality changes in their dementing dependants, lack of everyday conversation, criticism, excessive demands and difficult behaviour, such as aggression, disturbance at night, incontinence and wandering.

The way in which health and social care services are run locally can make all the difference to a carer's ability and desire to continue caring.

Carers generally value emotional support above all other types of help, but they also need information about the nature of the illness, the services available and how to gain access to them. They need contact with trusted professionals who can arrange for services to be provided, facilitate choice and assist with claiming benefits.

Identification and diagnosis of dementia[7,8]

It is important not to assume that cognitive impairment is dementia. A small proportion of people with dementia have an underlying abnormality and, when treated, show an improvement in cognitive function.

Diagnosis of dementia can be difficult because, although there are screening tools, there is no definitive test for dementia. Screening tests alone are insufficient to establish a diagnosis of dementia, and can lead to over-diagnosis.

A physical examination should exclude any underlying illness such as a stroke or Parkinsonism as the cause of the cognitive decline, so it is important to perform general health and neurological assessments. Enquire about other medication and the amount of alcohol consumed to eliminate these as causes of the apparent dementia. Investigation should be individualised according to the patient's situation, the severity of the condition and the social circumstances of the patient.

Physical investigations

A full dementia screen to identify coexisting conditions and exclude other causes of confusion may include the following:

- full blood count
- erythrocyte sedimentation rate (ESR)
- urea and electrolytes
- liver function tests (including gamma-glutamyl transferase)
- vitamin B_{12} and folate, if the mean corpuscular volume (MCV) is raised
- thyroid function test
- midstream urine
- vision and hearing (impairment of either may contribute to apparent cognitive impairment)
- electrocardiogram

- chest X-ray where indicated to exclude pneumonia or possible chest disease
- CT scan if symptoms are atypical, there is a recent head injury, clinical suspicion of an underlying tumour, new onset of fits, unexplained focal neurological signs, or antidementia drugs are being considered.

Mental state screening instruments

Tests that are widely used to assess cognitive impairment include the Mini-Mental State Examination (MMSE)[8] or the Abbreviated Mental-Test Score (AMT) version,[9] and the Six-Item Cognitive Impairment Test (6CIT).[10,11] A clock-drawing test is becoming increasingly popular and is usually used with the MMSE.[12]

The AMT provides a quick way to evaluate cognitive function in general practice in order to screen for dementia or monitor its progression. The AMT consists of a set of 10 questions for the patient, and it takes about 10 minutes to administer and complete. A cognitively intact person should answer the 10 questions correctly, whereas a score of less than 6 indicates cognitive impairment.

Box 7.2 The Abbreviated Mental Test Score[9]

Each correct answer scores one point.

1 Age.
2 Time to nearest hour.
3 An address to be repeated by the patient at the end of the test.
4 Year.
5 Name of hospital or residence, etc. where patient is staying.
6 Recognition of two individuals (e.g. doctor, home-help, etc.).
7 Date of birth.
8 Year in which First World War started.
9 Name of present monarch.
10 Count backwards from 20 to 1.

The MMSE consists of 30 questions covering four sections which include orientation to day, spelling WORLD backwards, recalling three words and writing a sentence.[7,8] Take all other factors into consideration when interpreting the result, including the patient's background, culture, education and social class, and information from their carers about how they are functioning.

Box 7.3

'GPs should be alert to early signs of memory problems, confusion or depression in their routine practice when older people, especially those over 75, consult them for any health problem.'[3]

Although the MMSE has its limitations, it represents a brief, standardised method by which cognitive mental status can be graded. It assesses orientation, attention, immediate and short-term recall, language, and the ability to follow simple verbal and written commands. Scoring allows the patient to be rated with regard to cognitive function, and the results of successive tests to be compared over time.

The Six-Item Cognitive Impairment Test (6CIT) consists of six questions that are simple and non-cultural, and which do not require any complex interpretation. GPs have found that the 6CIT is more appropriate for individuals with mild dementia than the MMSE.[11] The 6CIT can be loaded on the practice computer as a Windows-based program.

The clock-drawing test is another simple method for screening and assessing the severity of dementia,[12] as drawing a clock face can reveal deficits in parietal lobe function.

Some areas have memory clinics, some of which only see patients at an early stage of dementia, while others perform multidisciplinary assessments at any stage of dementia.

Box 7.4

A survey of 1000 GPs in England and Wales[3] found that:

- half of GPs believe that it is important to look for early signs of dementia
- two out of five GPs use protocols or tests such as the MMSE to diagnose dementia
- less than half of GPs believe that they have sufficient training to identify and manage dementia
- three out of four GPs believe that they have ready access to specialist services to help them to diagnose and manage dementia.

The importance of early diagnosis[3,12,13]

GPs and their practice teams are often criticised for the delay in diagnosing dementia and their inaction in arranging investigations, referral and social support when the condition is obvious. The medical profession as a whole needs to develop a positive approach to memory failure and its assessment and treatment.

Early diagnosis should allow the highest quality of life to be achieved for as long as possible through provision of support services, patient and carer counselling (so that they know what to expect) and early intervention with new drugs to delay cognitive decline.

In addition, early detection may lead to the detection and treatment of coexisting medical conditions that can be mistaken for dementia. These include drug side-effects, depression, some metabolic disorders and urinary tract infections. At later stages in the dementia these conditions may be more difficult to distinguish and treat.

The primary care team have a central role in the diagnosis and ongoing care of patients with dementia. Their roles in diagnosis and management include the following:

- identifying patients who have a suspected dementing illness
- excluding treatable causes
- referring patients to specialist psychiatric services when the diagnosis is uncertain
- providing information about the diagnosis and prognosis of dementia
- assessing the informal carer's ability to cope
- providing information about the available services and benefits
- helping with access to and co-ordination of a range of support services
- providing emotional support to informal carers
- treating co-existing conditions as they occur
- monitoring and co-ordinating care of the patient with dementia
- prescribing new drugs for dementia in association with the physician who is initiating treatment.

Dementia can only be managed if it has been identified. The Alzheimer's Disease Society advocates an early and accurate diagnosis. They argue that early diagnosis benefits not only the patient with the dementing illness, but also their carers. Knowing the diagnosis provides carers with an explanation for their relative's behaviour, and stops them blaming themselves or the relative.[13]

Providing a co-ordinated multidisciplinary local service

The majority of patients with dementia are identified at a late stage in the disease, usually following a medical or carer crisis. One reason that has been postulated for this is the scant formal training that GPs and other health professionals have received about the detection and management of dementia. The emphasis of published research about dementia has been on the epidemiology, genetics and neuropsychology of dementing illnesses. Many GPs still assume that cognitive decline is an inevitable part of ageing.

Box 7.5 Do you tell patients with dementia what their diagnosis is?

A minority of GPs (39%) always or often tell their patients that they have dementia, compared with 95% who always or often tell their patients the diagnosis when they have cancer. The authors of the study recommended that doctors' change in attitude towards being more open nowadays about disclosing a diagnosis of cancer to a patient should be extended to more openness in sharing the diagnosis of dementia with their patients, too.[14]

GPs need sufficient information, training and support to fulfil their role in the detection and management of patients with dementia. Working in a multidisciplinary team is a good way to learn more about the potential benefits of other agencies, as in the example shown in Box 7.6.

Box 7.6 One-stop dementia care set up in Glasgow[15]

The Co-ordination of Assessment and Resources in Dementia (CARD) project in Glasgow is provided by social services and primary care. All use a multidisciplinary needs assessment tool which is completed by patients with dementia and their carers. This has resulted in local initiatives being established to 'fast-track' personal care, equipment and adaptations to people's homes. The scheme has improved communication between health and social care services, and has enabled the targeting of resources at patients' needs in a co-ordinated way in order to plug gaps and avoid discontinuity of care and services.

Since the service was set up in 1995 it has assessed 400 patients with memory loss and includes all 21 practices in South-West Glasgow. The scheme enables vulnerable people with dementia to be managed at home rather than being admitted to hospital or other continuing care.

Step 1 – patient with suspected memory loss is referred to the scheme.
Step 2 – patient is screened with MMSE and for depression, and has routine blood tests.
Step 3 – patients with dementia undergo needs assessment, including finance, house care, health and mobility, social interaction, thinking and memory, self-care and toileting, behaviour and mental state.
Step 4 – informal carers are assessed with regard to the degree of stress they are experiencing.
Step 5 – multidisciplinary care plans are drafted at a team meeting, led by the care co-ordinator.
Step 6 – a full report and action plan are sent to the referring GP.
Step 7 – patient and carer(s) are reassessed at five-monthly intervals, when new unmet needs are addressed. Cognitive state is assessed annually.
Step 8 – patient's GP is kept informed of their progress.

The Audit Commission report[3] suggested that GPs should provide better information and support to patients and their carers. It recommended that doctors should screen carers for depression in order to ensure that their needs are not forgotten.

Treatment of dementia[1]

The North of England Evidence-Based Guidelines Development Project[16] and the Scottish Intercollegiate Guidelines Network[17] give similar recommendations for pharmacological treatments. Neuroleptic drugs are the mainstay of pharmacological treatment but they do have side-effects such as parkinsonism, drowsiness, tardive dyskinesia, falls, accelerating cognitive decline, and severe neuroleptic sensitivity reactions. Patients with Lewy body dementia are thought to be more sensitive to the side-effects of neuroleptic medication.

Pharmaceutical treatments for dementia are aimed at helping to modify behavioural and psychiatric disturbances and symptoms such as depression, delusions, hallucinations and wandering, and treating coexisting conditions such as incontinence. New drugs are being developed to slow cognitive decline.

Box 7.7

There seems to be an association between high levels of serum homocysteine and low levels of serum folate and dementia. The conclusion of one review was that taking a daily multivitamin is likely to prevent cardiovascular disease, cancer and possibly dementia.[18]

The past few years have seen more success in the treatment and management of Alzheimer's disease than in other types of dementia. Many pharmacological approaches have been abandoned due to their limited success and the severity of their adverse effects (e.g. ergoloid mesilates (gerimal, hydergine, niloric), chelation therapy, *N*-acetyl carnitine and lecithin).

Box 7.8

An extract of *Ginkgo biloba* (called EGb and now licensed in Germany) taken as a 40 mg tablet before each main meal seems to be effective for people with dementia and is well tolerated. The 'number needed to treat' (NNT) calculation predicts that about seven patients with dementia have to be treated with 120 mg of *Ginkgo* extract daily for one year for one of them to show an improvement which they would not have had with placebo treatment. That level of improvement is equivalent to a six-month delay in the progression of the dementia.[1,19]

Cholinesterase inhibitors

The most important advance is the development of second-generation cholinesterase inhibitors, which do not require frequent laboratory monitoring for hepatotoxicity as the first-generation cholinesterase inhibitors did.

Choline acetyltransferase activity is significantly reduced in Alzheimer's disease and is related to the severity of dementia. Correcting the cholinergic deficit is one logical approach to pharmacological intervention that is being developed.

Acetylcholinesterase inhibitors prevent the breakdown of acetylcholine, thus increasing the level of acetylcholine that is available to postsynaptic neurones.

Acetylcholinesterase inhibitors create potential improvements in memory and cognition by increasing the level of acetylcholine that is available at the synapse. In placebo-controlled studies, tacrine hydrochoride and donepezil hydrochloride have produced a modest slowing of cognitive and functional decline in some patients over time. A return to pre-treatment performance levels occurs when treatment is discontinued. No data are available on the long-term effects of acetylcholinesterase inhibitor therapy.

None of these cholinesterase inhibitor drugs have been shown to exert any effect on the quality of life of the patient with dementia.

Comparison of the relative efficacy of various antidementia drugs is limited by the fact that researchers have used different methods to diagnose dementia and to measure its progression, so that like cannot easily be compared with like. Similarly, there is little consensus about the meaningfulness of outcome measures from the perspectives of health and social care professionals, patients and carers. The rating scales used in the methods of screening and assessment that are employed by health professionals are not necessarily important to people with dementia and their carers.

Donepezil

Donepezil is well tolerated, and is more efective than placebo in 'improving cognitive function and global clinical state'.[1] It is rapidly absorbed from the gastrointestinal tract and has a high bioavailability and a long half-life (70 hours), with no reported hepatotoxic side-effects.

One-third of patients who were treated with donepezil and reviewed in one report showed a modest improvement in their overall condition, another third showed a decreased rate of cognitive decline, and the remainder showed no treatment response. There is no evidence that the use of donepezil prevents the progression of Alzheimer's disease.

GPs should not initiate treatment with donepezil.[16]

Rivastigmine

One large review found that the use of rivastigmine is associated with improved cognitive function in older people with Alzheimer's disease, but that nausea is common.

One trial of rivastigmine reported no serious adverse effects, but one-third of the patients who were taking the high dose withdrew from the study. The most commonly cited adverse effects were nausea (reported by 50% of those taking it) and vomiting (reported by one-third).

Thioridazine

Thioridazine is an antipsychotic or neuroleptic drug that has been used for decades. The risk of abnormal cardiac arrhythmias is so high that it should no longer be prescribed routinely. Patients who are on the drug should be prescribed a suitable alternative or have ECG screening every time doses are increased, and at six-monthly intervals.

Selegiline[1]

Selegiline is a monoamine oxidase inhibitor that is used in patients with severe parkinsonism. It is more effective than placebo in improving cognitive function, behavioural disturbance and mood in patients with Alzheimer's disease, but in one review there was no observed effect on clinical global state. Selegiline is well tolerated and has no serious adverse effects.

Non-pharmacological treatments

Non-pharmacological treatments can help to ameliorate behavioural problems and assist in the overall care of patients with dementia. There is a huge range of such treatments, beyond the scope of this chapter,[14,17] and they include the following:

- reality orientation
- behavioural intervention
- occupational activities
- environmental modification
- validation therapy
- reminiscence
- sensory stimulation.

Reflection exercise

Exercise 15 (for practice managers, GPs and practice nurses)

(i) Does your practice or agency have a register of patients with dementia and their carers?
If not, why not establish one? This will involve agreeing a protocol for screening and classifying individuals with regard to their type and degree of dementia.

(ii) If you do have a register, check its accuracy. How many patients have you classified with dementia and how have you done this? How does the number you have identified compare with the proportion of patients with dementia in an average practice, as cited earlier in this chapter?

(iii) Audit the care that patients registered with dementia have received in the last 12 months. Have they had an annual review? If so, did the GP or nurse check whether they were receiving sufficient practical support, assist them with claiming financial benefits, check that their current medication was justified and sufficient, and ensure that any treatable coexisting conditions were recognised and managed appropriately?

(iv) Audit the care that the carers of dementia have received in the previous 12 months. How does it compare with Standard 6 of the National Service Framework for Mental Health intended to apply to carers of those with severe mental illness (*see* Box 7.9)?

Box 7.9 Standard 6 of the NSF for Mental Health

All individuals who provide regular and substantial care for a person on the care programme approach (CPA) should:

- have an assessment made of their caring, physical or mental health needs, which is repeated on at least an annual basis
- have their own written care plan, which is given to them and implemented in discussion with them.

Now that you have completed this interactive reflection exercise, transfer the information about your learning needs to the relevant section in the empty template on pages 151–161 if you are working on your own personal development plan, or to the practice personal and professional development plan on pages 174–181 if you are working on a practice team learning plan. Don't forget to keep the evidence of your learning in your personal portfolio.

References

1 Barton S (ed.) (2001) *Clinical Evidence. Issue 5.* BMJ Publishing Group, London.

2 Coyle F (2000) Dementia. In: *Royal College of General Practitioners Members' Reference Book.* Royal College of General Practitioners, London.

3 Audit Commission (2000) *Forget Me Not: mental health services for older people.* Audit Commission, London.

4 Ely M, Melzer D, Opit L *et al.* (1996) Estimating the numbers and characteristics of elderly people with cognitive disability in local populations. *Res Policy Planning.* **14**: 13–18.

5 Medical Research Council (1998) Cognitive function and dementia in six areas of England and Wales. *Psychol Med.* **28**: 319–35.

6 Hofman A, Rocca WA, Brayne C *et al.* (1991) The prevalence of dementia in Europe: a collaborative study of 1980–1990 findings. *Int J Epidemiol.* **20**: 736–48.

7 Thistlethwaite J (2000) Dementia: the role of the primary care team. *Update.* **17 August**: 150–4.

8 Folstein MF, Folstein SE and McHugh PR (1975) Mini-Mental State: a practical method for grading the cognitive state of patients for the clinician. *J Psychiatr Res.* **12**: 189–98.

9 Research Unit of the Royal College of Physicians and the British Geriatrics Society (1992) *Standardised Assessment Scales for Elderly People.* The Royal College of Physicians of London and the British Geriatrics Society, London.

10 Brooke P and Bullock R (1999) Validation of the 6-item Cognitive Impairment Test. *Int J Geriatr Psychiatry.* **14**: 936–40.

11 Brooke P (2000) A better test for cognitive loss. *Practitioner.* **244**: 389, 463.

12 Sunderland T, Hill JL, Mellow AM *et al.* (1989) Clock drawing in Alzheimer's disease. A novel measure of dementia severity. *J Am Geriatr Soc.* **37**: 725–9.

13 Chapman A, Jacques A and Marshall M (1994) *Dementia Care: a handbook for residential and day care.* Age Concern, London.

14 Vassilas CA and Donaldson J (1999). Telling the truth: what do general practitioners say to patients with dementia or terminal cancer? *Br J Gen Pract*. **48**: 1081–2.

15 O'Neill K (2000) How one GP lifts the load of dementia. *Doctor*. **27 January**: 76–9.

16 Eccles M, Clarke J and Livingston M (1998) North of England Evidence-Based Guidelines Development Project: guideline for the primary care management of dementia. *BMJ*. **317**: 802–8.

17 Scottish Intercollegiate Guidelines Network (1998) *Interventions in the Management of Behavioural and Psychological Aspects of Dementia*. Scottish Intercollegiate Guidelines Network, Edinburgh.

18 Moore A, McQuay H and Muir Gray JA (1999) Folate, homocysteine and dementia. *Bandolier*. **6**: 1–2.

19 Moore A, McQuay H and Muir Gray JA (1998) Dementia diagnosis and treatment. *Bandolier*. **5**: 2–3.

CHAPTER 8

Draw up and apply your personal development plan

You may want to focus on the clinical management of mental health problems in general, or you may be interested in a specific condition such as dementia, or wish to look at stress management for yourself. A personal development plan (PDP) on either of these topics, or on other conditions, could form part of a practice personal and professional development plan (PPDP) on mental healthcare (*see* Chapter 9). We have included worked examples of personal development plans focused around stress management for health professionals themselves, and dementia, on pages 130–150.

As we explained in the introduction, you may decide to allocate 50% of the time you intend to spend drawing up and applying a personal development plan in any one year on learning more about mental healthcare. That would leave space in your learning plan for other important topics such as diabetes, coronary heart disease or cancer – whatever is a priority for you, your practice team and your patient population. There will be some overlap between topics, as you cannot consider a person with mental health problems in isolation from their general physical health and well-being.

The examples given are very comprehensive, and you may not want to include so much in your own personal development plan. You might include different topics and educational activities, because your needs and circumstances are different to those of the example practitioners here. You might move on to Chapter 9, and modify the example of a practice personal and professional development plan given there for your personal development plan.

Choose several methods to justify the topic you have chosen, or to identify your learning needs. Incorporate learning needs or baseline information from the 'Reflection exercises' at the end of each chapter, such as the clinical governance check-list from the material in

Chapter 1 or the SWOT analysis in Chapter 6. Transfer the information about your learning needs from any of the completed reflection exercises at the end of the chapters that are relevant to you, to the empty template of the personal development plan that follows on pages 151–161. The reflection exercises that you decide to select will depend on the focus of your personal development plan, as in the worked examples here.

Draft the action plan. You might already have prepared this in one of the reflection tasks at the end of each chapter. Show it to someone else and ask for their views as to whether it is relevant, well balanced and achievable. Plan and undertake your learning and demonstrate the subsequent improvements in your knowledge and practice.

Drawing up your personal development plan and carrying it out might take 10 to 40 hours depending on what topic you choose, the extent of preliminary needs assessment, how detailed your action plan is and the type of evaluation that you do.

Worked examples

Personal development plan focusing on dementia

Who chose the topic?

You may have chosen it yourself out of a personal interest in the care of elderly people. For example, a close family member might have developed Alzheimer's disease, or your practice or your primary care organisation (PCO) might have encouraged you to learn more about the topic for any of the reasons given below.

Why is the topic a priority?

(i) *A personal/professional priority?* You may realise that you are not up to date in developments in the management of dementia. You may have been unable to justify why you would not prescribe a new drug for dementia when asked to do so by the family of a patient with dementia.

(ii) *A practice priority?* You may be anticipating a new nursing home being opened in your locality and want to prepare for that eventuality.

(iii) *A district/national priority?* There are increasing numbers of elderly people in the population, of whom a considerable proportion will develop dementia.

Who will be included in your personal development plan?

You might include:

- GPs
- social workers
- practice nurses, district nurses, health visitors
- local psychiatrist
- practice manager
- community psychiatric nurse
- community pharmacist
- carers of those with dementia
- other agencies who might help (e.g. housing associations, Citizens' Advice Bureau).

You might find out more about each of their roles and responsibilities, or organise a multidisciplinary learning event, or simply be aware of who is who, and where you and patients can contact them in your locality.

What baseline information will you collect and how?

- Numbers of patients with dementia on your practice list. If your practice classifies people's conditions and enters them on the computer, then a simple search should yield the numbers. If you do not have a 'disease register', you may need to compile a list by hand with all practice staff contributing names. Map out how many patients live in residential or nursing homes and how many live in the community.
- Audit the extent of pro-active and reactive care received by patients with dementia. Find out how many have had their hearing and sight checked in the last two years or been reviewed to see whether they are incontinent and if so need help or aids.
- Identity of providers of health and social care for patients with dementia.
- Any information on morbidity or mortality of patients with dementia that your local public health department can supply.
- Any protocol or guide that is available either in the practice or in the district with regard to the assessment and management of dementia.
- Any literature for patients with dementia or their carers.
- Any survey or monitoring exercise that has been undertaken in the practice with regard to patients with dementia.

How will you identify your learning needs?

- You might hold a practice meeting with all of those involved in providing care as listed above and agree a more effective model for service delivery. They will have learning needs, too, associated with any newly allotted roles and responsibilities.
- Obtain feedback from the carers of those with dementia by simply asking them what you or the practice as a whole can do better.
- A significant event audit conducted on a patient with dementia who is taken to the Accident and Emergency department by exasperated neighbours and dumped there may reveal learning needs for you and the rest of the practice team.

What are the learning needs of the practice and how do they match your needs?

You may find that everyone in the practice realises that managing dementia more effectively is a priority for the practice, or you might find that you are on your own in wanting to learn more and change practice. You will need the commitment of the practice team if you are going to achieve any more than change your own management and practice.

Is there any patient or public input to your plan?

You could usefully ask the representative from the local branch of the voluntary Carers' Association or individual carers themselves for their views and suggestions for improvements in helping those with dementia to receive as much practical help as possible. You might do this by talking informally, holding a focus group, or organising an open evening with some education and networking, as well as gaining their input directly into your plans.

You or someone else from the practice might sit in on a meeting of a local voluntary organisation or neighbourhood forum where dementia is on the agenda. In this way you should pick up tips for what you need to learn.

How might you integrate the 14 components of clinical governance into your personal development plan focusing on the topic of dementia?

Establishing a learning culture: you might hold an open evening for carers of patients with dementia to discuss what practical help they need, using a question-and-answer format. You might invite a social worker or continence nurse to give a short talk.

Managing resources and services: knowing who else might provide practical and social care to those with dementia or their carers, what they can offer, where to find them and when (e.g. financial advisers in the local Citizens' Advice Bureau).

Establishing a research and development culture: you might critically appraise the latest key paper on prescription drugs for dementia.

Reliable and accurate data: make sure that you know how many people with dementia are registered with your practice and whether they live in the community. Are they on medication that might exacerbate their health problems? Look up the side-effects of the drugs they are taking.

Evidence-based practice and policy: find out and apply the evidence for selecting appropriate tests to classify an individual as having dementia. For instance, do you know whether you can use the Mini-Mental test in a primary care environment, or is it only intended for hospital out-patients?

Confidentiality: make sure that you know the rules about divulging confidential information about one person (the patient with dementia) to another (e.g. their carer or a volunteer in the community) without their express permission and informed consent.

Health gain: learning more about concurrent physical problems that occur in patients with dementia (e.g. urinary infections causing incontinence, undetected deafness) and treating those problems effectively will result in considerable health gains for the patients concerned.

Coherent team: understand everyone's roles and responsibilities in managing dementia effectively as a multidisciplinary team, and the capability of other members of the team of which you might previously have been unaware.

Audit and evaluation: audit the number of patients with dementia who are followed up in the practice, or undertake a significant event audit. You might audit adherence to a practice protocol for the management of dementia, identifying the gaps in care for which you are responsible and your associated learning needs.

Meaningful involvement of patients and the public: learn what methods can be used to engage patients with dementia or their carers in a meaningful way, so that they can influence decision making.

Health promotion: target carers for health promotion. Find out what problems they usually develop – caring for someone with dementia 24 hours a day is very stressful and can be depressing.

Risk management: learn more about reducing the risks of over-prescribing, or about keeping the patient safe from harm, such as that from elder abuse.

Accountability and performance: learn how to construct and present your 'portfolio of evidence' demonstrating that you are looking after patients with dementia along the lines laid out in the practice protocol or the good practice that you adopt.

Core requirements: could a different skill mix in your practice team provide more cost-effective care of patients with dementia? You may have to learn more about skill mix first.

Aims of your personal development plan after the preliminary data-gathering exercise:

To provide effective management of patients with dementia within currently available resources

and/or

to determine a more effective approach to providing care for patients with dementia in your practice

and/or

to learn more about the clinical management of patients with dementia and apply that learning in practice.

Action plan (include the objectives above, timetabled action and expected outcomes)

Who is involved?/What is the setting? You in the general practice setting and anyone else in the practice team, or associated with it, with whom you might work.

Timetabled action.   Start date: . . .

By 2 months: preliminary data-gathering completed and staff involved.
- Is there a practice protocol for managing patients with dementia?
- Numbers of staff; map expertise; list other providers.
- Referral patterns and prescribing patterns.
- Information about the characteristics of the practice population, known performance of providing care, local and national priorities.

By 4 months: review current performance.
- Extent of knowledge and usage of practice protocol for managing dementia; whether it is based on best practice and fits with others' management plans (e.g. hospital trust).
- Audit of actual performance according to pre-agreed criteria (e.g. assessing newly diagnosed patients).
- Compare performance with any or several of the 14 components of clinical governance.

By 6 months: identify solutions and associated training needs.
- Learn how to detect individuals with dementia earlier.
- Write or revise the practice protocol on the management of dementia, having searched for other evidence-based protocols; input from practice team and psychiatrist.
- Clarify your role and responsibilities for caring for patients with dementia.
- Apply the protocol, identify gaps in care, propose changes to others at practice meeting.
- Attend external course or in-house training as appropriate.

By 12 months: make changes.
- Feed back information to practice manager to relay to PCO in order to justify request for more resources.
- Improve access and find ways to prioritise patients with dementia.
- Increase referrals to voluntary sector.

Expected outcomes: more effective management of dementia, greater detection of concurrent problems from pro-active approach, reduction in over-prescribing, and increased help from those in voluntary sector.

How does your personal development plan tie in with your other strategic plans? (e.g. the practice's business or personal and professional development plans, or the Primary Care Investment Plan)

It should tie in with the practice's development plan and the PCO's development plan as far as possible. The PCO's plans should in turn match with the local health improvement programme (HImP), social services and other NHS trusts' strategic developments.

What additional resources will you require to execute your plan and from where do you hope to obtain them?

You might ask the practice to sponsor the costs of obtaining literature describing best practice. Your entitlement to reimbursement of course fees or time spent on education and training will depend on who you are/your post, and the terms and conditions in your contract. It will also depend on whether the practice perceives that dementia is a priority for the practice team and you are undertaking work on the practice's behalf.

How will you evaluate your personal development plan?

You could use similar methods to those which you used to identify your learning needs as given in the reflection exercises (e.g. you might re-audit a topic in which you believe you have made changes and improved your performance).

How will you know when you have achieved your objectives?

You can re-audit the care and services you have focused on 12 months later that relate to the objectives you defined at the outset.

How will you disseminate the learning from your plan to the rest of the practice team and patients? How will you sustain your new-found knowledge or skills?

You might share what you have learned at the local Carers' Association members' meeting, at a practice educational meeting for the rest of the practice team, or by writing an article for the medical, nursing or health management journal on effective management of dementia in primary care.

How will you handle new learning requirements as they crop up?

Jot down any thoughts you have about what else you need to learn as you discover it – or you will not be able to remember what it was you were going to look up later on.

Check out whether the topic you have chosen to learn is a priority and the way in which you plan to learn about it is appropriate

---

Your topic: *Dementia*

How have you identified your learning need(s)?

(*a*) PCO requirement   ☒   (*e*) Appraisal need   ☐

(*b*) Practice business   ☐   (*f*) New to post   ☐
     plan

(*c*) Legal mandatory   ☐   (*g*) Individual decision   ☐
     requirement

(*d*) Job requirement   ☒   (*h*) Patient feedback   ☒

                                    (*i*) Other   ☐

Have you discussed or planned your learning needs with anyone else?

Yes   ☒   No   ☐   If yes, who? *Other colleagues.*

What are your learning need(s) and/or objective(s) in terms of the following?

Knowledge. What new information do you hope to gain to help you to do this?

To learn more about when to start treatment with newly developed drugs.

Skills. What should you be able to do differently as a result of undertaking this learning in your development plan?

Identify individuals suffering from dementia earlier on in the course of their illness.

Behaviour/professional practice. How will this impact on the way in which you subsequently do things?

I might become the 'expert' in our practice about dementia, and use assessment tests for patients whom any member of the practice team suspects has dementia.

Details and date of desired development activity: *Within 3 months: attend a day course locally on managing dementia. Within 6 months: sit in on a dementia assessment clinic with a local consultant specialising in elderly care, spend a few hours at a local day centre that caters for those with dementia and talk to social carers; undertake more reading. Prepare the learning and achievements for my next job appraisal.*

Details of any previous training and/or experience that you have in this area/dates:
Nil, I'm ashamed to say!

What is your current performance in this area compared with the requirements of your job?

Need significant development in this area	☐	Need some development in this area	☒
Satisfactory in this area	☐	Do well in this area	☐

What is the level of job relevance that this area has to your role and responsibilities?

Has no relevance to job	☐	Has some relevance	☐
Relevant to job	☐	Very relevant	☒
Essential to job	☐		

Describe how the proposed education/training is relevant to your job:
Integral part of my work caring for elderly people.

Do you need additional support in identifying a suitable development activity?

Yes ☒   No ☐

What do you need?
To know when and where relevant courses are being held. Help in learning to search the literature for key papers.

Describe the differences or improvements for you, your practice, PCO or employing NHS trust as a result of undertaking this activity:
My newly found expertise will be useful to others, I shall be raising the standards of care that we offer to patients with dementia in our

practice, and I shall be more aware of what help and support other agencies can offer patients, referring them as appropriate.

Assess the priority of your proposed educational/training activity:

Urgent ☐   High ☒   Medium ☐   Low ☐

Describe how the proposed activity will meet your learning needs rather than any other type of course or training on the topic:

The mix of learning from a day's course and personal learning by observing others' everyday practice in different settings should help me to identify what I don't know and meet my learning needs.

If you had a free choice, would you want to learn this?   Yes/No

If **No**, why not? (please circle all that apply):

Waste of time
I have already done it
It is not relevant to my work or career goals
Other

If **Yes**, what reasons are most important to you? (put them in rank order)

To improve my performance	1
To increase my knowledge	3
To get promotion	
I am just interested in it	
To be better than my colleagues	
To do a more interesting job	2
To enable me to be more confident	4
Because it will help me	

Record of your learning about dementia

You would add the date, length of time spent, etc., for each learning activity

	Activity 1 – knowledge of best practice in management of dementia	Activity 2 – learning skills of identifying and classifying patients with dementia	Activity 3 – more aware of help and support services from non-NHS agencies	Activity 4
In-house formal learning	CPN runs an hour session on dementia one lunch-time with input from a carer as well			
External courses	Day course at local postgraduate centre	Covered at local day course (*see* Activity 1)		
Informal and personal	Sit in with hospital consultant in dementia clinic Reading and reflecting	Discuss criteria used with hospital consultant and staff in dementia clinic; use their assessment scales that are relevant to primary care Reading	Spend time observing in day centre Talk to social care workers Read literature from voluntary sector and social services	
Qualifications and/or experience gained	Experiences of others at course, and other initiatives in the literature	Experience of secondary care procedures	Experience of social care centres	

Personal development plan focusing on stress management

What is the topic?

Stress management – for self.

Why is the topic a priority?

(i) *A personal and professional priority*? After working in the health service for 20 years, I realise that my job satisfaction is being whittled away by the stresses I am experiencing at work from the many demands that are made on me. I think that the effects of this stress are starting to threaten the quality of my everyday work.

(ii) *A practice priority*? Someone under stress affects all members of the practice team. This may be because the stressed person creates more work for others if their performance is below par (e.g. due to being forgetful or making mistakes), or stress may result in their being resistant to any change.

(iii) *A district priority*? The PCO is encouraging more awareness of the need for and benefits of good stress management in general practice.

(iv) *A national priority*? The government is emphasising the importance of good human resource management in the quality and well-being of the NHS work-force.

Who will be included in my personal plan?

Although my personal development plan is focused on my needs, I cannot 'beat' stress without significant changes in the organisation of the practice. Therefore I will invite others to join in my initiative as it evolves, either by learning to control stress for themselves or by involving them in reorganising the practice systems that create stress. The following will be included:

- GPs
- practice manager
- practice nurses
- reception staff
- practice secretary
- family and partner at home.

What baseline information will I collect?

Causes and effects of stress on me at work, and outside work.

How will I identify my learning needs?

- Audit of my everyday practice (e.g. significant event audits of several unexpected demands, such as extra patients, or interruptions – whatever crops up over a couple of days).
- Observation of my practice – by using a stress log diary and self-assessment scores of perceived stress, and by informal comments from others.
- Observation of stressors in my life outside work – by using a stress log diary, and by informal comments from others.
- Comparing the methods of stress management I know about with the list of possibilities given in a manual on stress management (*see* Chapter 5).
- Group discussion in a practice meeting attended by GPs and employed and attached practice staff, where the general topic of 'stress at work' is debated. Should learn more about causes of stress for me by listening to what others find stressful and hearing more about their concerns and feelings.
- From previous appraisals.

What are the learning needs of the practice and how do they match my needs?

The practice will benefit if I am less stressed as an individual, as I will then be more likely to take a lead or actively support changes to improve practice systems and procedures. If I learn to control some of the stresses on me, this should have additional benefits for others in the practice team, as I should be easier to work with, more efficient and a better communicator.

I shall have to be careful that my suggestions for improving the practice organisation reduce stress levels for everyone whenever possible. If I simply control stress upon myself by redirecting demands on others who do not have the time, training or inclination for absorbing those demands, then I will be implementing my personal development plan at the expense of the overall good of the practice, which is untenable.

Is there any patient or public input to my plan?

I will use any informal feedback from patients, or any formal patient complaint about the practice, if it is relevant to me. That information might form the basis for a significant event audit. Unsolicited patient feedback might identify pressures in the practice that were previously unknown to me, or make me think about the causes or effects of stress for me, from which I might learn (e.g. remarks about punctuality, problems in obtaining help or advice).

Aims of my personal development plan arising from the preliminary data-gathering exercise

To reduce stress at work by:

- identifying three significant sources of stress for me at work that are within my ability to control either as an individual or working with others in the practice
- learning how to recognise causes of stress and their effects on me
- learning more about methods of stress management appropriate for the stressors I have identified and how to apply them
- learning how improving practice systems and procedures might be possible, and how to involve others in the practice team in such reorganisation.

How I might integrate the 14 components of clinical governance into my personal development plan focusing on stress management

Establishing a learning culture: meeting with another colleague who is doing his or her own personal development plan, to swap notes and encourage each other.

Managing resources and services: controlling key sources of stress such as reducing the impact of patients who need to be seen on the same day as 'urgent' cases, or reducing interruptions.

Establishing a research and development culture: conducting a survey to identify sources of stress, or compare levels of demand before and after introducing an intervention.

Reliable and accurate data: becoming more competent at operating the practice computer may be one possible solution to reducing stress, revealed by the preliminary needs assessment.

Evidence-based practice and policy: updating my knowledge of the evidence for best practice for common clinical conditions may relieve feelings of guilt and uncertainty that have been causing me stress, or reduce the potential for making mistakes.

Confidentiality: re-registering as a patient with a nearby practice where my medical details will be confidential; some colleagues have access to my records in the practice where I work.

Health gain: reducing stress will result in fewer physical symptoms of stress and associated medication such as analgesics, indigestion remedies, etc.

Coherent team: good communication between myself and the others in the practice team should reduce stress for all of us – perhaps through a news-sheet when changes are expected.

Audit and evaluation: audit will be part of the learning needs assessment as described; the (hopefully) beneficial effects of any intervention will be evaluated.

Meaningful involvement of patients and the public: seeking patients' views through focus groups (for instance) might help us to improve access so that I find better ways of managing patients and consequently am not under such time pressure when they seek my help.

Health promotion: as I learn what works for me in managing stress, I might ensure that similar help is available to promote stress reduction for patients (e.g. relaxation tapes).

Risk management: using a risk assessment, reduction and management approach to my personal safety in the practice or on home visits should identify, avoid or minimise risk factors which threaten my safety (and that of others) and provoke stress.

Accountability and performance: being under too much stress for too long will inevitably make me less effective; this should be reversible with good stress management.

Core requirements: I am more likely to adopt new approaches that are more cost-effective if I am less stressed and more willing to embrace change.

Action plan

Who is involved?/What is the setting? Me in the general practice setting and anyone else in the practice team or associated with it, with whom I work.

Timetabled action. Start date: . . .

By 2 months: preliminary data-gathering completed and any others involved in initiative.
• Is there a practice protocol for managing stress?
• Map expertise in practice (e.g. community psychiatric nurse, practice nurse with counselling skills) and list other providers of help (e.g. British Medical Association stress counselling service, local helpline).
• Baseline information about sources of stress from completed stress diaries.

By 4 months: review current performance.
- Audits of actual performance via pre-agreed criteria (e.g. number of interruptions while working in surgery, number of 'extra' patients attending in addition to booked surgeries).
- Compare performance with any or several of the 14 components of clinical governance described on the previous page.

By 6 months: identify solutions and associated training needs.
- Learn new skills – in assertiveness, time management and delegation.
- Write or revise the practice protocol on stress management – to include health surveillance, and monitoring sources of stress at work.
- Clarify my role in the practice organisation – be more definite so that I know what my responsibilities are and will not feel guilty if others do not fulfil their duties for which I am not responsible.
- Apply the practice protocol for stress management, identify gaps, and propose changes to others at the practice meeting.
- Attend external courses or in-house training as appropriate.
- Visit another practice to see how they have combated their stressors.

By 12 months: make changes.
- Feed back information to the practice team about what is needed to reduce stress for me and for the others prior to making changes (e.g. set up more opportunities for mutual support).
- Improve efficiency of practice organisation – from patients' and staff perspectives.
- News-sheet once every quarter describing any changes in practice protocol or people's roles and responsibilities.
- Training for other staff who will be taking on new roles.
- Find a 'buddy' outside the practice with whom to discuss progress with our personal development plans.
- Re-register with a nearby practice with a GP in whom I have complete trust who is independent of my own practice.

Expected outcomes: more effective control of sources of stress; more efficient practice organisation; better teamwork, including communication and delegation; more effective performance at work; more willing to consider and implement change.

How does my learning plan tie in with other strategic plans?

It will tie in with the practice's development plan and the PCO's development plan as far as possible. The PCO's plans should in turn fit with the local health improvement programme (HImP), social services and other NHS trusts' strategic developments. All of these organisations encourage the finding of ways to manage stress at work more effectively.

What additional resources will I require to execute my plan and from where do I hope to obtain them?

I will ask the practice to sponsor the costs of obtaining relaxation tapes for patients, and I shall use them, too. I would expect to be able to attend a stress management course during my working day.

How will I evaluate my learning plan?

I will use similar methods to those I used to identify my learning needs as given earlier – that is, keep other stress logs of the pressures I perceive at work and outside work, and re-audit interruptions and relevant aspects of the practice organisation (e.g. appointment times) after we have made changes and improved the practice organisation. I shall discuss with my 'buddy' how they think I am progressing with my personal development plan.

How will I know when I have achieved my objectives?

I shall re-audit and monitor my stress levels by means of a diary as described above, 12 months later. I shall determine whether I am using more effective coping methods to minimise any sources of stress that I have not been able to obliterate. I shall review my progress at my next job appraisal or clinical supervision session.

How will I disseminate the learning from my plan to the rest of the practice team and patients? How will I sustain my new-found knowledge or skills?

I shall share what I have learned at the peer support meeting I have set up in the practice for other team members. I shall also encourage the rest of the practice team to adopt 'health at work' for a practice personal and professional development plan, or at least for it to be the topic of an educational meeting for all of the practice team. I shall write an article for the medical, nursing or health management press on effective stress management in primary care!

How will I handle new learning requirements as they crop up?

I shall jot down any thoughts about what else I need to learn about managing stress as I discover it – or I will not be able to remember what it was I was going to look up or think more about later on.

Check whether the topic you have chosen is a priority and the way in which you plan to learn about it is appropriate

---

Your topic: *Stress management*

How have you identified your learning need(s)?

(*a*) PCO requirement   ☐   (*e*) Appraisal need   ☐

(*b*) Practice business   ☐   (*f*) New to post   ☐
     plan

(*c*) Legal mandatory   ☐   (*g*) Individual decision   ☒
     requirement

(*d*) Job requirement   ☐   (*h*) Patient feedback   ☒

                                 (*i*) Other   ☒

Have you discussed or planned your learning needs with anyone else?

Yes ☒   No ☐   If yes, who? *My 'buddy' with whom I am discussing progress with my personal development plan, and the practice manager.*

What are your learning need(s) and/or objective(s) in terms of the following?

Knowledge. What new information do you hope to gain to help you to do this?

Sources of stress; effective methods of stress management.

Skills. What should you be able to do differently as a result of undertaking this learning in your development plan?

Be more assertive; learn to delegate without putting strain on others; introduce change to practice systems so that the organisation is more efficient.

Behaviour/professional practice. How will this impact on the way in which you subsequently do things?

My performance at work should improve.

Details and date of desired development activity:

Attend stress management course that covers a range of coping methods next week.

Details of any previous training and/or experience that you have in this area/dates:

Have read widely on the topic; have discussed the topic with the community psychiatric nurse over a cup of coffee.

What is your current performance in this area compared with the requirements of your job?

Need significant development in this area	☒	Need some development in this area	☐
Satisfactory in this area	☐	Do well in this area	☐

What is the level of job relevance that this area has to your role and responsibilities?

Has no relevance to job	☐	Has some relevance	☐
Relevant to job	☐	Very relevant	☒
Essential to job	☐		

Describe how the proposed education/training is relevant to your job:

Reducing stress should help me to improve my concentration and performance in almost every aspect of my job. It should help my home life, too, if I am less distracted by stress and jobs I have brought home because I seem to be so inefficient at work.

Do you need additional support in identifying a suitable development activity?

Yes ☐   No ☒

Describe the differences or improvements for you, your practice or the PCO as a result of undertaking this activity:

Everyone in the practice and patients should benefit from the new improved version of me when under less stress. They should also benefit if I introduce changes in the practice systems that reduce stress for others and not just for me. The patients and the PCO may notice that the practice is working more effectively.

Assess the priority of your proposed educational/training activity:

Urgent ☐　　　High ☒　　　Medium ☐　　　Low ☐

Describe how the proposed activity will meet your learning needs rather than any other type of course or training on the topic:

It is local so I won't waste time in travelling. It is interactive small group work, so I should benefit from hearing about others' ways of controlling stress at work.

If you had a free choice, would you want to learn this?　<u>Yes</u>/No

If **No**, why not? (please circle all that apply):

Waste of time
I have already done it
It is not relevant to my work or career goals
Other

If **Yes**, rank the reasons that are applicable to you in order of importance:

To improve my performance	1
To increase my knowledge	4
To get promotion	
I am just interested in it	
To be better than my colleagues	
To do a more interesting job	
To enable me to be more confident	2
Because it will help me	3
Other	

Record of my learning about stress management (mid-way through completion of personal development plan)

	Activity 1 – dealing with stress at work	Activity 2 – time management	Activity 3 – increasing support to beat stress	Activity 4 – identifying stressors and sources of pressure
In-house formal learning	Community psychiatric nurse ran one-hour session on dealing with post-traumatic stress, after a member of staff died in a road accident.		Organised first one-hour meeting at lunchtime to discuss setting up regular support forum, facilitated by local lay counsellor.	
External courses	One-day course at nearby postgraduate centre, small group learning – included several stress management methods.	Learned about time management at the same one-day course (see Activity 1).	Learned about support from one-day course (of Activity 1).	
Informal and personal	Chat with practice staff over coffee, in corridors, etc.	Spent two hours in another practice as part of training activities. Gained new ideas on time management from their practice manager.	Read up on the topic from a good manual on the subject. Did some of the interactive exercises.	Fed audit results back to GPs, practice manager and staff at practice meeting. Led discussion on what we shall do about the problem areas – to submit action plan. Interesting discussion afterwards.
Qualifications and/or experience gained?	Certificate for one-day course.	Experience gained from comparing my practice with the other practice.		

Reflection and planning exercise

Now complete your own personal development plan. It might be focused on a different topic to *dementia* or *stress management*. It might be your personal perspective of the worked example of the practice personal and professional development plan focused on *depression,* described in the next chapter. Or you might choose to tackle mental healthcare as a whole.

Photocopy the template of a personal development plan that is given below, or complete the version in the book. Choose a topic that meets your individual needs.

Template for your personal and professional development plan

Photocopy the following pages and complete one chart per topic.

What topic have you chosen?

Justify why this topic is a priority:

A personal and professional priority?

A practice priority?

A district priority?

A national priority?

Who will be included in your personal development plan?
(Anyone other than you? Other GPs, employed staff, attached staff, others from outside the practice, patients?)

What baseline information will you collect and how?

How will you identify your learning needs?
(How will you obtain this and who will do it? Self-completion check-lists, discussion, appraisal, audit, patient feedback? Look back to the reflection exercises at the end of each chapter).

What are the learning needs of the practice and how do they match your needs?

Is there any patient or public input to your personal development plan?

How might you integrate the 14 components of clinical governance into your personal development plan focusing on the topic of . . . . ?

Establishing a learning culture:

Managing resources and services:

Establishing a research and development culture:

Reliable and accurate data:

Evidence-based practice and policy:

Confidentiality:

Health gain:

Coherent team:

Audit and evaluation:

Meaningful involvement of patients and the public:

Health promotion:

Risk management:

Accountability and performance:

Core requirements:

Objectives of your personal development plan arising from the preliminary data-gathering exercise:

Action plan (include timetabled action and expected outcomes)

How does your personal development plan tie in with your other strategic plans?
(For example, the practice's business or development plan or the Primary Care Investment Plan?)

What additional resources will you require to execute your plan and from where do you hope to obtain them?
(Will you have to pay any course fees? Will you be able to organise any protected time for learning in working hours?)

How will you evaluate your personal development plan?

How will you know when you have achieved your objectives?
(How will you measure success?)

How will you disseminate the learning from your plan to the rest of the practice team and patients? How will you sustain your new-found knowledge or skills?

How will you handle new learning requirements as they crop up?

Check whether the topic you have chosen is a priority and the way in which you plan to learn about it is appropriate

Photocopy this proforma for future use.

Your topic:

How have you identified your learning need(s)?

(a) PCO requirement ☐   (e) Appraisal need ☐

(b) Practice business ☐   (f) New to post ☐
    plan

(c) Legal mandatory ☐   (g) Individual decision ☐
    requirement

(d) Job requirement ☐   (h) Patient feedback ☐

    (i) Other ☐

Have you discussed or planned your learning needs with anyone else?

Yes ☐   No ☐   If yes, who?

What are your learning need(s) and/or objective(s) in terms of the following?

Knowledge. What new information do you hope to gain to help you to do this?

Skills. What should you be able to do differently as a result of undertaking this learning in your development plan?

Behaviour/professional practice. How will this impact on the way in which you subsequently do things?

Details and date of desired development activity:

Details of any previous training and/or experience you have in this area/dates:

What is your current performance in this area compared with the requirements of your job?

Need significant ☐   Need some ☐
development in this area   development in this area

Satisfactory in this area ☐   Do well in this area ☐

What is the level of job relevance that this area has to your role and responsibilities?

Has no relevance to job ☐   Has some relevance ☐

Relevant to job ☐   Very relevant ☐

Essential to job ☐

Describe how the proposed education/training is relevant to your job:

Do you need additional support in identifying a suitable development activity?

Yes ☐   No ☐

If Yes, what do you need?

Describe the differences or improvements for you, your practice or your PCO as a result of undertaking this activity:

Assess the priority of your proposed educational/training activity:

Urgent ☐   High ☐   Medium ☐   Low ☐

Describe how the proposed activity will meet your learning needs rather than any other type of course or training on the topic:

If you had a free choice, would you want to learn this?   Yes/No

If **No**, why not? (please circle all that apply):

Waste of time
I have already done it
It is not relevant to my work or career goals
Other

If **Yes**, what reasons are most important to you? (put them in rank order):

To improve my performance
To increase my knowledge
To get promotion
I am just interested in it
To be better than my colleagues
To do a more interesting job
To enable me to be more confident
Because it will help me
Other

Record of your learning

Write in the topic, date, time spent and type of learning

	Activity 1	Activity 2	Activity 3	Activity 4
In-house formal learning				
External courses				
Informal and personal				
Qualifications and/or experience gained				

CHAPTER 9

Draw up your practice personal and professional development plan

The practice personal and professional development plan (PPDP) should cater for everyone who works in the practice. Clinical governance principles will balance the development needs of the population, the practice, the PCO *and* the individual personal development plans (PDPs) of your practice team.

You might want to start by asking everyone to identify their own learning needs, combining them with those of other people and then checking them against the practice business plan. Alternatively, you could start from the other direction, by developing a practice-based personal and professional development plan from your business plan and then identifying everyone's individual learning needs within that. Whichever direction you start from, you must ensure that you integrate team members' individual needs with those of your practice and the needs and directives of the NHS.

Make your learning plan flexible – you may want to add something in later when circumstances suddenly change or an additional need becomes apparent, perhaps as a result of a complaint, the launch of a new drug or new requirements from the government, the PCO or the National Institute for Clinical Excellence (NICE).

Long-term locums (longer than six months, say), assistants, retained doctors and salaried GPs should all be included in the practice plan. Remember to include all those staff who work for the practice, however few their hours – you cannot manage without them or they would not be there!

Time is one of the resources that must be considered when drawing up your action plan. Adequate resources must be in place for your learning needs, and protected time must be built in.

Read the worked example through. It is not intended to be prescriptive, but merely a guide to the types of techniques that you might use to identify your learning needs, define your objectives, undertake an assessment against the 14 components of clinical governance, and plan your action and evaluation. Then turn to the empty template that follows and start to complete that by transferring the information you have gathered from the range of reflection exercises at the end of each chapter in the book.

Worked example

Practice personal and professional development plan focused on depression

Who chose the topic?

You may have chosen it as a practice team, or there may be one member of the practice staff who champions the topic and gains everyone else's agreement to address it.

Justify why this topic is a priority:

(i) *A practice and professional priority?* Missed depression can mean that the patients concerned are treated for their associated physical symptoms for a considerable time. This may be costly in terms of the quality of patients' lives as well as unnecessary investigations and treatments. If these patients are off work with undetected and untreated depression, the social and economic costs to their families will be significant.

(ii) *A district priority?* Yes. Many district health improvement programmes (HImPs) have made improving mental healthcare a priority.

(iii) *A national priority?* Yes. 'Depression' is a key feature in the National Service Framework for Mental Health for England and the vision for health improvement in the other three countries in the UK.

Who will be included in the practice personal and professional development plan?

The following might be included:

- the community psychiatric nurse (practice attached or NHS trust employed)
- practice nurses
- GPs

- the practice manager
- receptionists
- practice secretaries
- community pharmacists
- counsellors (voluntary, Relate, practice employed)
- health visitors
- district nurses
- social workers from the local patch
- any interested psychologist or psychiatrist.

Who will collect the baseline information and how?

You might ask for information on the practice population from the public health service – your practice secretary might send for this. You might run a computer search for medication or other audit of the records – your receptionist or computer operator might do this.

Where are you now? (baseline)

This might include the following points.

- Description of practice population (numbers, age and gender) and numbers of patients newly diagnosed with depression in the last 12 months. If you cannot retrieve this information in a computerised form, you may have to keep prospective records for three months instead.
- Comparison of prescribing of different types of antidepressants – between prescribers in your practice, and between the practice and other practices. You might obtain anonymised prescribing data comparing your performance with that of others from the local prescribing adviser. Referral patterns in the last 12 months (to the community psychiatric nurse, to counsellors, to psychologists, to practice staff (practice nurse, health visitor), to psychiatrists and to voluntary sector organisations). Compare referral behaviour both between practitioners and with other practices. The health authority and hospital trusts may be able to supply you with comparative data.
- Patient survey – have you undertaken such a survey in relation to depression or to services in general? If so, what did the results show? You might look at factors such as satisfaction with explanation, and doctor or nurse listening to the patient.
- Audit – have you undertaken one recently that would be relevant to 'depression'? If not, you might look at compliance with treatment (e.g. average duration for which patients took medication such as antidepressants, or 'did not attend' figures for referrals to others).

- Performance indicators held by the health authority or PCO – do they hold any relevant data on file such as numbers and reasons for complaints?
- Numbers and types of staff with relevant expertise in your team. You might map out all of those who are practice team members or to whom you can refer patients (their particular skills and the range of help offered). Do you know all of the possible sources of help in the voluntary sector and what their qualifications and expertise are?

What information will you obtain about individual learning wishes and needs?

- The prescribing adviser may have visited the practice to discuss GPs' over- or under-prescribing of antidepressants.
- A significant event (e.g. the suicide of a young man) should set the team reviewing whether any more might have been done to treat his depression.
- You might hold a practice team discussion to elicit people's concerns and their perceptions of the main issues for the practice both as individuals and as an organisation. Collect their ideas for solutions. The practice nurse might organise this session.
- All members of the team might complete a check-list enquiring about their perceived learning needs, and might suggest the learning needs of other members of the team.
- Clinicians might be aware that they need to learn more about depression as a priority, having discussed it with their clinical supervisor (nurse), educational tutor (GP) or at a recent job appraisal or clinical supervision session.

What are the learning needs for the practice and how do they match the needs of the individual?

Individuals may wish to specialise. For example, the practice nurse may wish to undertake an accredited course in counselling. The nurse's aspirations may match the needs of the practice. For instance, it may be that a practice nurse with more expertise in counselling may replace lost community psychiatric nurse (CPN) time or meet the needs of a cohort of newly registered refugees who have been housed in your area. However, it may be that the practice nurse training would be better targeted at other clinical topics as you already have an adequate number of trained counsellors among the practice team.

Is there any patient or public input to your plan?

You might ask patients with depression about their care and their ideas for improvements, and seek feedback on how you are doing. You might consult your patient panel if you have one, to ask them for feedback about access and the appointment system, or for suggestions about priority issues that you might tackle. You might include one or two patients who have suffered from depression, or their carers, to participate in in-house training for staff, to convey the patient perspective so that your staff and services become more patient centred.

How will you prioritise everyone's needs in a fair and open way?

You might gather all of the available information and make it available to anyone working in the practice who is interested. You could then decide on the appropriate action at a designated team meeting which a representative of the nurses, GPs, practice staff and the practice manager attend.

What are the aims of the practice personal and professional development plan arising from the preliminary data-gathering exercise?

1   To apply the evidence for best practice in managing depression in a systematic way.
2   To learn about and use screening tools for depression.

How might you integrate the 14 components of clinical governance into your practice personal and professional development plan focusing on 'depression'?

Establishing a learning culture: design the practice personal and professional development plan through a democratic process; involve all relevant professionals (including the community psychiatric nurse and community pharmacist) in practice-based teaching and learning.

Managing resources and services: control the way in which the resources for training are allocated according to service-relevant needs; alter referral patterns according to an agreed practice-based protocol for managing depression.

Establishing a research and development culture: encourage all practice staff to critically appraise the practice protocol and suggest changes to achieve more effective management of depression.

Reliable and accurate data: agree on a way of recording different types of depression, to which all staff adhere (e.g. use Read codes); consistent entry on computer for every case seen.

Evidence-based practice and policy: monitor adherence to the practice protocol for managing depression; individuals should justify any deviation from the practice protocol.

Confidentiality: increase awareness of issues surrounding the release of information about a person's mental health to others, with and without their permission; consider a policy to be implemented when patients are so ill and a danger to themselves that it may be ethical to release information without their permission.

Health gain: increase staff awareness of the frequency with which mental ill health presents with physical symptoms; increase staff expertise in detecting new cases of depression.

Coherent team: clearly agree roles and responsibilities in the management of depression, with everyone working within their areas of competence.

Audit and evaluation: review the success of the programme to take account of the context and setting as well as the clinical expertise and flexibility of the practice team to respond to unexpected events such as a new model of delivery of care to depressed patients.

Meaningful involvement of patients and the public: realise that questionnaires are an inappropriate medium for gathering information from people with moderate or severe mental health problems; develop more meaningful methods such as informal interviewing. Involve people with depression in decision making about alternative options for treatment.

Health promotion: screen patients for depression; target high-risk groups such as those individuals who have had strokes.

Risk management: anticipate those at risk of attempting suicide and take preventative action whenever possible; reduce missed diagnoses of depression through improved expertise of all staff (clinicians and receptionists).

Accountability and performance: use a mix of the factors in this example to obtain a more complete picture of your performance.

Core requirements: include time and support for members of the practice team to prevent their becoming depressed or burnt out in response to the volume of work, frequent changes and competing service demands.

Action plan

Who is involved?/What is the setting? All staff in practice team.

Timetabled action.   Start date: . . .

By 3 months: preliminary data-gathering completed and staff involved.
- Develop a protocol for managing patients with mild, moderate and severe depression.
- Numbers of staff; map expertise completed; list other providers.
- Referral patterns and prescribing patterns.
- Information about characteristics of the practice population, known performance, and local and national priorities.
- Staff complete check-lists giving views and suggestions.

By 5 months: review current performance.
- Extent of knowledge and usage of practice protocol for managing depression; whether it is based on best practice and fits with others' management plans (e.g. hospital trust).
- Access to appointments, telephone advice – audit of actual performance according to pre-agreed criteria.
- Compare performance with any or several of the 14 components of clinical governance.

By 7 months: identify solutions and associated training needs.
- Set up new systems for appropriate triage of priority patients.
- Write or revise the practice protocol on the management of depression, having searched for other evidence-based protocols; input from practice team and psychiatrist.
- Agree on the roles and responsibilities of the team for delivering care and services.
- Apply the protocol, and identify gaps in care, and proposed changes to delivery of care or services, so that GPs and nurses adhere to protocol.

- Certain staff attend external courses. The community pharmacist provides some in-house training on prescribing to GPs. Receptionists have in-house training on triage.
- Liaise with GP co-operative to review how GP deputies and nurses triage calls from or about those with depression. If there is a widespread learning need, contact the GP tutor to request a series of district-based seminars.

By 12 months: make changes.
- Feed back information to the PCO and mental health trust to justify request for resources.
- Improve access; find ways to prioritise patients with depression and other mental health problems; improve security of records and confidentiality of patients' medical details.
- Community pharmacist helps to review repeat prescribing.
- Increase referrals to the voluntary sector.
- Arrange a session from the Citizens' Advice Bureau in the practice to help patients to claim benefits of which they might otherwise have been unaware.
- Petition social services and the PCO for a practice-attached social worker; in the mean time, improve access to a named social worker at the local social services premises.

Expected outcomes: more effective management of depression; better patient compliance with medication and attendance at referrals; more flexible access arrangements; increased help from social services and financial advisers.

How does your practice personal and professional development plan tie in with your other strategic plans?

The management of depression should be a priority for the practice business plan if a great deal of effort is to be expended on improving the care and services of patients with depression as described in your practice personal and professional development plan.

What additional resources will you require?

Resources for training, and for changing prescribing and referral patterns (this might be an extra cost justified by health gains, or cost savings). You will have to readjust current resources or seek additional support from your PCO. If it is a priority in the district or the PCO's strategic plans, you may be able to tap into any additional resources that are available.

How much protected time will you allocate to staff to undertake the learning described in your plan?

This will depend on your circumstances, aspirations and needs. Staff entitlement to time off or reimbursement of course fees, etc., will depend on their contract and on the priority value that the practice or PCO places on their contribution to the development plan.

How will you evaluate your practice personal and professional development plan?

You might undertake an audit of any of the aspects of care and services that have featured so far.

You might use a SWOT analysis, but you will have had to anticipate its use in evaluation by undertaking the analysis as a baseline assessment and then reviewing progress at the time of completion of the initiative.

You might undertake a survey of patient satisfaction or compliance with treatment, before and after your initiative, using patients who are currently suffering from depression – that is, two separate groups of patients, so long as you have got the first lot better!

How will you know when you have achieved your objectives?

By using the audit and survey methods described above and measuring deviation from the agreed practice protocols.

How will you disseminate the learning from the plan to the rest of the practice team and patients? How will you sustain the new-found knowledge and skills?

You might write about it in a practice newsletter. Let all of the staff know at practice meetings what progress has been made. You might want to talk about your provision at a voluntary group meeting or at a neighbourhood forum. You might want to describe your success at a PCO meeting.

Pass on your skills and knowledge to others as required, and review your protocol at set intervals to incorporate new information.

How will you handle new learning requirements as they crop up?

The practice manager who leads the initiative can collate suggestions, complaints and observations as they are made by staff or patients in response to the new systems. The practice manager and clinical supervisor may revisit the topic of depression in annual appraisals to check on progress and any perceived new learning requirements.

Record of practice team learning about 'depression'

You would add the date, length of time spent, etc., for each learning activity

	Activity 1 – more rational prescribing	Activity 2 – prioritising high-risk patients	Activity 3 – awareness of non-NHS helping agencies	Activity 4 – revise practice protocol on management of depression
In-house formal learning	Health authority prescribing adviser held a small group session to review prescribing patterns of each GP partner, and compare the practice with others.	Practice team event to which practice manager and GP presented update on depression – signs and symptoms, risk management, and ideas on systems and procedures to improve access.		Final practice protocol described and explained at practice team event (see Activity 2). All roles and responsibilities of GPs, nurses, receptionists and practice manager agreed.
External courses	Prescribing was one topic in day's update course on 'depression' at local postgraduate centre.			GPs and practice nurse attended day's update course on depression.
Informal and personal	Two GPs read up on the topic and worked together to review prescribing in the practice protocol on the management of depression. Practice nurse joins in online discussion group debating best practice.	Practice nurse stuck newspaper cutting up on staffroom noticeboard of 'traffic-light' system used on medical records of patients known to be at high risk in another practice.	Manager of Citizens' Advice Bureau, officer from MIND and Relate counsellor all visit practice for half an hour at coffee-time to meet staff informally and tell team members about their services.	GP, practice nurse and practice manager drafted practice protocol in preparation for other team members to comment on it.
Qualifications and/or experience gained?		Practice manager visited another practice in the PCT to see how receptionists spot high-risk patients and arrange urgent access there.	One practice nurse decides to train to be a Relate counsellor as a 'volunteer'.	

Reflection and planning exercise

Now build up and complete your practice personal and professional development plan. It might be focused on a different topic to depression. It might tackle mental healthcare as a whole. Then you can mesh the personal development plans of everyone else in the practice team.

Photocopy the template of a practice personal and professional development plan that is given below, or complete the version in the book. Choose a topic that meets your individual practice needs.

The practice manager or a GP with responsibility for education might take a lead in this exercise. They will have to lead and motivate the team, anticipate skill needs for any planned changes in the way in which you will be delivering mental healthcare, and organise appropriate education and training in good time.

- Ensure that there are good communications within the practice about the learning plan.
- Organise regular staff meetings and separate educational meetings with team members and GPs. Invite attached staff to attend as appropriate.
- Be prepared to listen to staff and seek their involvement in changes.
- Agree protocols in clinical and organisational work practices and adhere to them.
- Monitor performance regularly and appraise staff. Move away from a blame culture, and use mistakes as learning opportunities (try anyway!).

Drawing up your practice personal and professional development plan and carrying it out might take from 10 to over 100 hours depending on what topic you choose, the extent of preliminary needs assessment, how many staff are involved and whether you include the time they spend in learning, how detailed your action plan is and the type of evaluation that you do.

Template for your practice personal and professional development plan

Photocopy the following pages.

What topic have you chosen?

Who chose it?

Justify why this topic is a priority:

A personal or professional priority?

A practice priority?

A district priority?

A national priority?

Who will be included in the practice personal and professional development plan?
(Anyone other than you? Other GPs, employed staff, attached staff, others from outside the practice, patients?)

What baseline information will you collect and how?

How will you identify your learning needs?
(How will you obtain this and who will do it? Self-completion check-lists, discussion, appraisal, audit, patient feedback?)

What are the learning needs of the practice and how do they match your needs?

Is there any patient or public input to your practice personal and professional development plan?

What are the aims of your practice personal and professional development plan arising from the preliminary data-gathering exercise?

How might you integrate the 14 components of clinical governance into your practice personal and professional development plan focusing on the topic of . . . . **?**

Establishing a learning culture:

Managing resources and services:

Establishing a research and development culture:

Reliable and accurate data:

Evidence-based practice and policy:

Confidentiality:

Health gain:

Coherent team:

Audit and evaluation:

Meaningful involvement of patients and the public:

Health promotion:

Risk management:

Accountability and performance:

Core requirements:

Action plan (include timetabled action and expected outcomes)

How does your practice personal and professional development plan tie in with your other strategic plans?
(e.g. the practice's business or development plan, the Primary Care Investment Plan or the health improvement programme?)

What additional resources will you require to execute your plan and from where do you hope to obtain them?
(Will you have to pay any course fees? Will you be able to organise any protected time for learning in working hours?)

How will you evaluate your practice personal and professional development plan?

How will you know when you have achieved your objectives?
(How will you measure success?)

How will you disseminate the learning from your plan to the rest of the practice team and patients? How will you sustain your new-found knowledge or skills?

How will you handle new learning requirements as they crop up?

Record of your learning

Write in the topic, date, time spent and type of learning

	Activity 1	Activity 2	Activity 3	Activity 4
In-house formal learning				
External courses				
Informal and personal				
Qualifications and/or experience gained				

Support groups, information and resources, and self-help literature about mental healthcare

Support groups, information and resources

Action on Addiction, Unit B, 3/1 Park Place, 12 Lawn Lane, London SW18 1UD. Tel: 020 7793 1011. Website: www.charitiesdirect.com

African-Caribbean Mental Health Association, 49 Effra Road, Suite 37, London SW2 1BZ. Tel: 020 7737 3603.

Alcohol Advisory Service, 309 Grays Inn Road, London WC1X 8QF. Tel: 020 7530 5900.

Alcohol Concern, Waterbridge House, 32–36 Loman Street, London SE1 0EE. Tel: 020 7928 7377. Website: www.alcoholconcern.org.uk

Alcoholics Anonymous, PO Box 1, Stonebow House, Stonebow, York YO1 7NJ. Tel: 01904 644026. Helpline: 0345 697555. Website: www.alcoholics-anonymous.org.uk

Alzheimer's Disease Society, Gordon House, 10 Greencoat Place, London SW1P 1PH. Tel: 020 7306 0606. Helpline: 0845 300 0336 (8 a.m.–6 p.m.)

Association for Brain-Damaged Children and Young Adults, Clifton House, 3 St Paul's Road, Foleshill, Coventry CV6 5DE. Tel: 01203 665450 (Monday to Friday 9.30 a.m.–3 p.m); 01203 581353 (24 hour).

British Association for Counselling (BAC), 1 Regent Place, Rugby CV21 2PJ. Tel: 01788 578328.

British Association of Psychotherapists, 37 Mapesbury Road, London NW2 4HJ. Tel: 020 8452 9823.

British Association for Sexual and Relationship Therapy, PO Box 62, Sheffield S10 3TL. www.basrt.org.uk

Carers National Association, 20–25 Glass House Yard, London EC1A 4JT. Tel: 020 7490 8818. Website: www.carersnorth.demon.co.uk

Child Death Helpline, c/o Bereavement Services Co-ordinator, Great Ormond Street Children's Hospital, London WC1N 3JH.
or The Alder Centre, Alderhay Children's Hospital, Eaton Road, Liverpool L12 2AP. Tel: 0800 282986 (freephone).

Childline, Freepost 1111, London N1 0BL. Helpline: 0800 1111.

Cleveland Rape and Sexual Abuse Counselling Service, PO Box 31, Middlesborough TS4 2JJ. Tel: 01642 223885.

Compassionate Friends, 53 North Street, Bristol, BS3 1EN. Tel: 0117 966 5202. Helpline: 0117 953 9639.

CRUSE Bereavement Care, Cruse House, 126 Sheen Road, Richmond TW9 1UR. Tel: 020 8940 4818; Fax: 0208 940 7638. Bereavement line: 0208 332 7227 (Monday to Friday 9.30 a.m.–5.00 p.m.).

Depression Alliance, 35 Westminster Bridge Road, London SE1 7JB. Tel: 020 7633 0557. Website: www.depressionalliance.org
A self-help network and for relatives who want help.

Depressives Anonymous, 36 Chestnut Avenue, Beverley HU17 9QU. Tel: 01482 860619.
An organisation run as a source of support for sufferers. Can put enquirer in contact with local groups.

Drinkline, First Floor Cavern Court, 8 Matthew Street, Liverpool L2 6RE. Helpline: 0800 917 8282. Dial & Listen: 0500 801802. Website: www.wrecked.co.uk

Drugaid, 16 Clyve Street, Caerphilly CF83 1GE. Tel: 029 2088 1000.

Eating Disorders Association, First Floor, Wensum House, 103 Prince of Wales Road, Norwich NR1 1DW. Tel: 01603 619090. Helpline: 01603 621414.

Enable, Sixth Floor, 7 Buchanan Street, Glasgow G1 3HL. Tel: 0141 226 4541.

Fellowship of Depressives Anonymous (FDA), Box FDA, Self-Help Nottingham, Ormiston House, 32–36 Pelham Street, Nottingham NG1 2EG. Information line: 01702 433838.

First Steps to Freedom, 7 Avon Court, School Lane, Kenilworth CV8 2GX. Tel: 01926 864473. Helpline: 01926 851608.

Gamblers Anonymous, PO Box 88, London SW10 0EU. Helpline: 020 7384 3040 (24 hours).

Hyperactive Children's Support Group, Sally Bunday, Secretary, 71 Whyke Lane, Chichester PO19 2LD. Fax: 01903 734726.

Institute for the Study of Drug Dependence, 32–36 Loman Street, London SE1 0EE. Tel: 020 7928 1211. Website: www.drugscope.org.uk

Institute of Family Therapy, 24–32 Stephenson Way, London NW1 2HX. Tel: 020 7391 9150.

Manic-Depression Fellowship, 8–10 High Street, Kingston upon Thames KT1 1EY. Tel: 0208 974 6550; Fax: 0208 974 6600.
and
Workspace, 23 New Mount Street, Manchester M4 4DE. Tel: 0161 953 4105. The Manic-Depression Fellowship educates the public about bipolar illness and publishes its own journal and newsletters. It runs self-help groups, open meetings and a pen-friend scheme.

MENCAP, 123 Golden Lane, London EC1Y 0RT. Tel: 020 7454 0454. Website: www.mencap.org.uk

Mental Health Foundation, 20/21 Cornwall Terrace, London NW1 4QL. Tel: 020 7535 7400.

MIND, Granta House, 15–19 Broadway, London E15 4BQ. Tel: 020 8519 2122. National helpline: 0345 660163. Website: www.mind.org.uk
MIND makes information available about most matters to do with mental health. The organisation is open to users, carers, family and friends, researchers, students, service providers and the public. Enquirers can be directed to local support groups.

National Autistic Society, 393 City Road, London EC1V 1NG. Tel: 020 7833 2299. Helpline: 020 7903 3555.

National Family Mediation, 9 Tavistock Place, London WC1H 9SN. Tel: 020 7383 5993. Website: www.nfm.u-net.com

National Phobics Society, c/o The Zion Community Resource Centre, 339 Stretford Road, Hulme, Manchester M15 4ZY. Tel: 0870 770 0456. Website: www.phobics-society.org.uk

National Schizophrenia Fellowship (NSF), 28 Castle Street, Kingston upon Thames KT1 1SS. Tel: 020 8547 3937. Head office: 30 Tabernacle Street, London EC2A 4DD. Tel: 020 7330 9100. Fax: 020 7330 9102. Helpline: 020 8974 6814. Website: www.nsf.org.uk
The NSF provides support, services and information, and it influences local, regional and national policies.

NHS Direct Online., Provides help and advice on conditions and treatment available to the public. Website: www.nhsdirect.nhs.uk

No Panic, 93 Brands Farm Way, Telford TF3 2JQ. Tel: 01952 590005. Helpline: 01952 590545 (10 a.m.–10 p.m.). Information Line: 0800 783 1531.

Postnatal depression – sources of help

Association for Post-Natal Illness (APNI), 25 Jerdan Place, Hammersmith, London SW6 1BE. Tel: 0207 386 0868.
The APNI has a network of telephone and postal volunteers who have suffered from postnatal illness and who offer one-to-one information, support and encouragement.

Meet-a-Mum Association (MAMA), Waterside Centre, 26 Avenue Road, South Norwood, London SE25 4DX. Tel: 020 8771 5595; Fax: 020 8239 1153. Helpline: 020 8768 0123 (Monday to Friday, 7 p.m.–10 p.m.). E-mail: Meet-A-Mum.Assoc@cableinet.co.uk
MAMA aims to alleviate feelings of loneliness and depression in the postnatal period. It is a charity and co-ordinates a series of self-help groups.

National Childbirth Trust, Alexandra House, Oldham Terrace, London W3 6NH. Tel: 0208 992 8637.

CRY-SIS, BM Cry-sis, London WC1N 3XX. Tel: 0207 404 5011. www.our-space.co.uk/serene/htm
CRY-SIS uses local voluntary counsellors who have experienced similar problems to offer help and support for parents whose children cry excessively, have a sleep problem, or have temper tantrums or other behavioural difficulties.

Parentline, Endway House, The Endway, Hadleigh, Benfleet SS7 2AN. Tel: 01702 554782. Helpline: 01702 559900.
Parentline is a voluntary self-help organisation that offers confidential support to parents under stress. A network of local telephone helplines is operated by trained parents. The organisation can also put parents in touch with local support groups.

Relate Marriage Guidance, Herbert Gray College, Little Church Street, Rugby CV21 3AP. Tel: 01788 573241. Website: www.relate.org.uk

Release – the National Drugs and Legal Helpline, 388 Old Street, London EC1V 9LT. Advice line: 020 7729 9904 (Monday to Friday 10 a.m.–6 p.m.). Emergencies: 020 7603 8654 (24 hours).

Samaritans, 10 The Grove, Slough SL1 1QP. Tel: 01753 532713. National helpline: 0345 909090.
A national organisation that offers support to those in distress who feel suicidal or despairing and need someone to talk to. Their phone lines are open 24 hours a day, every day of the year. The number of the local branch can be found in the telephone directory or obtained from the telephone operator.

SANE, First Floor Cityside House, 40 Alder Street, London E1 1EE. Tel: 020 7375 1002. National helpline: 0345 678000. Website: www.sane.org.uk This organisation provides information and support for carers, sufferers and friends.

Scottish Association for Mental Health, Cumbrae House, 15 Carlton Court, Glasgow G5 9JP. Tel: 0141 568 7000.

Seasonal Affective Disorder Association, PO Box 989, London SW7 2PZ. Tel: 01903 814942.

Sleep Council, High Corn Mill, Chapel Hill, Skipton BD23 1NL. Tel: 01756 791089. Website: www.sleepcouncil.org.uk

SmithKline Beecham Pharmaceuticals, Customer Response Centre, Mundells, Welwyn Garden City AL7 1EY. Tel: 0808 100 2228. Fax: 0808 100 8802. Email: ukpharma.customer@sb.com

Teachers' Advisory Council on Alcohol and Drug Education, 1 Hulme Place, The Crescent, Salford, Manchester M5 4QA. Tel: 0161 745 8925. Website: www.tacade.com

Tourette Syndrome (UK) Association, First Floor Offices, Old Bank Chambers, London Road, Crowborough TN6 2TT. Tel: 01892 669151.

Further reading

Books and guidelines for health professionals

Guidelines from ICD-10 Primary Health Care (*International Classification of Diseases* (10e), for Primary Healthcare), revised July 1995. In: Goldberg D, Gask L, Jenkins R (eds) *et al.* (2000) *WHO Guide to Mental Health Care.* Royal Society of Medicine, London.

Jackson G, Kassianos G, Koppel S and Nutt D (2000) Depression: a guide to its recognition and management in general practice. *Guidelines.* **11**: 1171–4.

Wilkinson G, Moore B and Moore P (2000) *Treating People with Depression. A practical guide for primary care.* Radcliffe Medical Press, Oxford.

Wilkinson G, Moore B and Moore P (2000) *Treating People with Anxiety and Stress. A practical guide for primary care.* Radcliffe Medical Press, Oxford.

Useful self-help books on dementia

The Mental Health Foundation publishes booklets about dementia, and on caring for people with dementia. For contact details, *see* page 185.

Useful self-help books on depression

Atkinson S (1993) *Climbing Out of Depression: a practical guide for sufferers.* Lion Publishing, Oxford.

Burns DD (1998) *Feeling Good: the new mood therapy.* New American Library.

Gillett R (1991) *Overcoming Depression: a practical self-help guide to prevention and treatment.* Dorling Kindersley, London.

Greenberger D and Padesky C (1995) *Mind Over Mood: change how you feel by changing the way you think.* Guilford Press, New York.

Harris TA (1973) *I'm OK, You're OK.* Pan Books, London.

Milligan S and Clare A (1993) *Depression and How to Survive It.* Arrow, London.

Rowe D (1996) *Depression: the way out of your prison.* Routledge, London.

Skynner R and Cleese J (1994) *Families and How to Survive Them.* Mandarin, London.

Useful self-help books on postnatal depression

Dix C (1985) *The New Mother Syndrome: coping with postpartum stress and depression.* Doubleday, London.

Marshall F (1993) *Coping with Postnatal Depression.* Sheldon Press, London.

Welburn V (1980) *Postnatal Depression.* Manchester University Press, Manchester.

Welford H (1998) *Postnatal Depression.* The National Childbirth Trust in association with HarperCollins, London.

Useful self-help books on schizophrenia

The National Schizophrenia Fellowship and The Mental Health Foundation publish a variety of factsheets and other literature. For contact details, *see* page 185.

Index